Praise for

THE ABUNDANCE LOOP

*"Juliana Park's **The Abundance Loop** is a deep meditation upon feeling grateful for having enough—such a powerful and liberating message during these complex economic times."*

— **Dacher Keltner**, faculty director,
Greater Good Science Center, UC Berkeley

*"**The Abundance Loop** is a simple yet powerful framework to kick you out of scarcity mode and into the discovery of real joy."*

— **Chip Conley**, *New York Times* best-selling author of
Emotional Equations and founder, Joie de Vivre

"Juliana Park is a rising thought leader who creatively integrates psychology, money, and spirituality to help you discover your true wealth."

— **Denise Brosseau**, author of *Ready to Be a Thought Leader?*
and CEO, Thought Leadership Lab

"When I work in the developing world on global health challenges, I see how little it takes for people to be happy. Juliana's work to shift people's mind-set from scarcity to abundance is exactly what we need to create increased self-worth and happiness in individuals."

— **Seema Handu, Ph.D.**, Chief Operating Officer,
Project Happiness

*"**The Abundance Loop** offers wise principles for creating abundance in our lives and enhancing our understanding of the relationship between personal growth and financial security. Juliana Parks invites readers to inquire into their fears and misconceptions about prosper-ity, and proposes a model of financial de   ～⁺ that includes self-knowledge, self-empowerment, appre⸱ gratefulness, generosity, and living fr*

— **Vernice Solimar, Ph.D.**, chair,
and Leadership Studies, John F.

D1042724

THE
ABUNDANCE
LOOP

HAY HOUSE TITLES OF RELATED INTEREST

YOU CAN HEAL YOUR LIFE, the movie,
starring Louise Hay & Friends
(available as a 1-DVD program and an expanded 2-DVD set)
Watch the trailer at: www.LouiseHayMovie.com

THE SHIFT, the movie,
starring Dr. Wayne W. Dyer
(available as a 1-DVD program and an expanded 2-DVD set)
Watch the trailer at: www.DyerMovie.com

*DESTRESSIFYING: The Real-World Guide to Personal Empowerment,
Lasting Fulfillment, and Peace of Mind*, by davidji

*DON'T LET ANYTHING DULL YOUR SPARKLE: How to Break Free
of Negativity and Drama*, by Doreen Virtue

EXPERIENCE YOUR GOOD NOW! Learning to Use Affirmations,
by Louise Hay

*MIRACLES NOW: 108 Life-Changing Tools for Less Stress, More Flow,
and Finding Your True Purpose*, by Gabrielle Bernstein

*MONEY: A Love Story: Untangle Your Financial Woes and
Create the Life You Really Want*, by Kate Northrup

THE WAY OF THE HAMMOCK: Designing Calm for a Busy Life,
by Marga Odahowski

WISHES FULFILLED: Mastering the Art of Manifesting,
by Dr. Wayne W. Dyer

All of the above are available at your local bookstore,
or may be ordered from:

Hay House USA: www.hayhouse.com®
Hay House Australia: www.hayhouse.com.au
Hay House UK: www.hayhouse.co.uk
Hay House South Africa: info@hayhouse.co.za
Hay House India: www.hayhouse.co.in

THE ABUNDANCE LOOP

8 Steps to Manifest Conscious Wealth

Juliana Park, CFP®

HAY HOUSE, INC.

Carlsbad, California • New York City
London • Sydney • Johannesburg
Vancouver • Hong Kong • New Delhi

Published and distributed in the United States by: Hay House, Inc.: www .hayhouse.com® • *Published and distributed in Australia by:* Hay House Australia Pty. Ltd.: www.hayhouse.com.au • *Published and distributed in the United Kingdom by:* Hay House UK, Ltd.: www.hayhouse.co.uk • *Published and distributed in the Republic of South Africa by:* Hay House SA (Pty), Ltd.: info@hayhouse.co.za • *Distributed in Canada by:* Raincoast Books: www.raincoast.com • *Published in India by:* Hay House Publishers India: www.hayhouse.co.in

Interior design: Pamela Homan • *Interior illustrations:* JP Mixed Media

Library of Congress Cataloging-in-Publication Data

Park, Juliana, date.
  The abundance loop : 8 steps to manifest conscious wealth / Juliana Park.
    pages cm
  ISBN 978-1-4019-4374-5 (paperback)
  1. Money--Psychological aspects. 2. Wealth--Psychological aspects. 3. Wealth--Religious aspects. 4. Conduct of life. 5. Spiritual life. I. Title.
  HG222.3.P37 2015
  332.024'01--dc23
                                        2015008914

Tradepaper ISBN: 978-1-4019-4374-5

10 9 8 7 6 5 4 3 2 1
1st edition, July 2015

Printed in the United States of America

SUSTAINABLE FORESTRY INITIATIVE
Certified Chain of Custody
Promoting Sustainable Forestry
www.sfiprogram.org
SFI-01268
SFI label applies to the text stock

*To Mom and Chris,
for reminding me
that I matter.*

CONTENTS

INTRODUCTION

In Pursuit of True Abundance

Wherever I am, I love asking people a simple question: "What does abundance mean to you?"

I hear many different answers, from men and women, and they seem to have little to do with age, socioeconomic status, or cultural background. Some simply say that abundance means not having to worry about bills. Others say it's to have freedom, to have enough money to do what they want, to start their own business, or to travel the world. And there are those who feel that abundance is having more than enough so they can share it with their loved ones.

To some, abundance doesn't have to do with money in the bank; they see an abundant life as one full of joy, connecting with family and friends, being outdoors in nature, and continually learning. What about good health? Yes, I also hear this answer, as well as being accepted, loved, and respected.

Just about any time I engage people in a conversation about abundance, they speak up, their postures straighten, and their faces light up. Each person defines abundance in his or her own unique way, but the net feeling is the same. We let out a collective "ahhhh" as we experience the peace that comes from envisioning our bounty.

But just watch what happens when we start to talk about *money.* Suddenly the energy changes. Relaxation quickly dissipates and tension takes over. When most of us think about our relationship to money, we feel "ugghh."

I wrote *The Abundance Loop* to help you stop feeling "ugghh" and get you to "ahhhh." As you work along with me through the eight steps, which I'll explain in the following pages, I aim to help you achieve both financial security and spiritual serenity, so you can experience the freedom to create the life you truly want.

Throughout this book, you will find two common threads: the fear of not *having enough* and, more important, the fear of not *being enough*. In the chapters to come, I will challenge your beliefs about what is possible and guide you to take clear actions that will increase both your net worth and self-worth.

When Is It Enough?

Since 2002, I have served as a financial advisor at a major Wall Street firm. I help families accumulate, preserve, and transfer their wealth so they can achieve their retirement, education, philanthropic, and estate-planning goals. I noticed that even with significant financial wealth, some people can easily succumb to the belief that "there's never enough."

Whether unemployed or steadily earning more than $1 million a year, whether they have $10,000 in debt or $10 million in assets, people can feel inadequate. No matter how much *I* earned, I also felt inadequate way too often.

I realize now that my view of the world and of myself was shaped by my childhood. Growing up in a Korean household in a middle-class neighborhood in the United States, I believed that as long as I followed directions, I would be fine. So, I went to the "right" schools, worked at the "right" jobs, crafted the "right" résumé, and married the "right" man. But along the way, I didn't feel "right." Meeting other people's expectations made me feel valuable, but I grew tired of giving myself away and letting others determine my worth. I was afraid of speaking my truth because I didn't believe it mattered. I didn't believe *I* mattered.

Then in 2009, I could finally see how my own feelings of fear and inadequacy not only were holding me back financially and personally, but were also affecting my health. I met with a breath practitioner, a life coach who specifically helps clients to access their emotions through breathwork. I live in the San Francisco Bay Area, where I have access to many kinds of wonderful healers, and this one in particular helped me to see that I was not taking full breaths. I was holding in so much fear that it was obstructing something as fundamental to my life as breathing.

When she asked me what I was missing in my life, what I truly wanted, I simply replied that I wanted to achieve the freedom to live an authentic life. I knew it sounded vague, but honestly, at the time, it was all I could say. I didn't even know where this idea came from or what it actually meant. I just felt emotionally and physically constricted from speaking my truth and expressing my authentic self.

With a great deal of support from my counselors and close friends, I began to make some tough decisions and life changes that were better for me, my health, and my family. But even after my divorce in 2010, more questions kept coming up: *Who was I and what did I want? Why did I dismiss my own needs and wants for so many years? Why did I spend my days helping others find true wealth while I ignored my own?*

What's Holding You Back?

I worked with a number of coaches, therapists, and healers to help me answer these questions. Given all the time and money I was spending on self-actualization, I figured I might as well get a degree in it. I decided to go to graduate school at John F. Kennedy University School of Holistic Studies, where I immersed myself in psychology and consciousness classes that directly impacted my personal growth and transformation. I had been seeking someone to answer my questions, and although many tried to help me, I ultimately had to develop the tools to free myself. Through journaling my thoughts and meditating on a daily basis, I gradually learned how to increase my awareness and I realized that the issue wasn't my job, my relationships, or a lack of knowledge about money. Beneath the various obstacles preventing me from living my best life, the real culprit was *fear.*

It took me quite a while to understand my intense fears and my defensive patterns, but eventually, as I stayed with the process, I began to see why I made the choices I did and how those choices trapped me in scarcity. Gradually, I garnered wisdom from spiritual teachers and practices, and I integrated those with my own experiences in life, finance, art, and psychology. The result is a simple, yet effective, framework to help manifest abundance.

This insight came in the form of two "loops," which I have called the *Scarcity Loop* and the *Abundance Loop.* Almost as soon as I began to share these concepts with friends, with colleagues, and in workshops I led, I started getting positive feedback. Many people have told me how reframing their lives through the lens of the Abundance Loop has brought them peace of mind about who they are and what they have. And, just as significant, this framework has guided them to change their behaviors to achieve better outcomes not only in their finances, but also with their career paths, health, partners, and friends, as well as their own emotions.

By understanding and consistently practicing the eight steps in this book, you will witness a shift in your relationship to money, with others, and most important, with yourself. You will be able to clarify what is driving your choices and know how to take conscious action to manifest what abundance means to you.

I truly believe *The Abundance Loop* will bring you to a place of "ahhhh" in your daily life, where you are at peace with all that you have and all that you are. It's time to break out of scarcity and move toward your divine abundance!

How to Get the Most from This Book

I've structured *The Abundance Loop* into eight steps that will help you manifest conscious wealth. These steps are the ABCs of abundance, but to make them easier for you to remember, each step starts with a letter *c* word, such as *choose, clarify, connect,* and so on. I encourage you to keep an open mind as you dive into these ideas, and I recommend that you read this book from beginning to end, keeping a journal or your laptop by your side.

Take your time and gently go through the questions, stories, and exercises with love and compassion for yourself. The process of transforming your mind-set from scarcity to abundance can bring up feelings of anxiety, which you'll naturally be inclined to resist. Keep in mind that you already hold the source of abundance within you, and the eight-step process offered here will uncover what is rightfully yours. I applaud you for finding the courage to invest in yourself so you can create a life that reflects who you truly are . . . *abundant!*

As you begin the steps, you will notice that I have included personal questions intended to get you to inquire more deeply and practical exercises to help you make the most of each step. You will also find many true stories, some from my own life and some about people I know. From time to time, I also created composite characters by combining traits and behaviors from multiple people in order to protect their identities.

— In **Step 1**, I explain in detail how the Scarcity Loop and the Abundance Loop came about and how they work. I guide you to clarify which loop you are living in and to understand the fascinating relationship between financial terminology and spiritual equivalents, so you can apply this foundational knowledge to the other seven steps.

— As you move on to **Step 2**, I will challenge your current limiting beliefs and work with you to raise your awareness. You will discover who you really are and rewrite the script running through your head so you can break unhealthy patterns and pave the way for abundance.

— This prepares you for **Step 3**, where I will help you recognize and appreciate the many resources you do have in your life and show you why it's vital to be thankful for even the little things. By cultivating gratitude and clarifying what matters to you, you will plant your thoughts and actions in fertile soil and learn to nurture them so that financial and spiritual wealth can grow.

— The information and exercises in **Step 4** will help you clarify your values and intentions. Identifying your deepest values is critical, and this is a central theme throughout the rest of the book, for they serve as the touchstone for you to manifest your divine purpose.

— In **Step 5**, you will learn to calculate your many resources, both financial and spiritual, some of which I bet you aren't even aware of. This step's exercises will help you take inventory of what you have; what you owe; and what you are doing with your money, time, and energy—instilling within you a full sense of your net worth and your self-worth.

— Once you have these first five steps under your belt, **Step 6** ups the challenge and invites you to commit to conscious action. Developing a strong conviction about your divine purpose will guide you to choose the right kinds of conscious action.

— **Step 7** takes this further and explains how to connect and collaborate with others to co-create the reality you truly want.

— Finally, in **Step 8**, it's time to celebrate the freedom to be your true self, welcoming abundance in all the ways that are important to you. You will find that once you have shifted your mind-set and your behavioral patterns to align with what you really want, you will enjoy financial and emotional peace. Indeed, most people report feeling an increased sense of freedom, empowerment, and joy once they master these skills.

Specifically, you will be able to shift from being a consumer to an investor, assess your net worth and your self-worth, and learn how to increase them both, along with your cash flow and energy flow. Ultimately, you can experience deep contentment that comes with constructing a well-balanced plan for your money, and the peace of mind that you have enough and that you *are* enough. With consistent practice, you can renew your relationship to money and yourself in ways that allow for financial and spiritual prosperity.

While this all sounds good, be aware this is *not* a get-rich-quick or get-happy-quick book. Creating abundance takes patience and diligence. You will continue to go back and forth between the loops, but over time, it will become easier to discern when you are getting stuck in the Scarcity Loop again, and you will know what to do to reboot yourself toward the Abundance Loop using the techniques you practiced when you first implemented the program.

So let's get started!

STEP 1

Choose to Break Free from Scarcity

Earlier in my life, I wasn't conscious of how much I was spending or the debt I was incurring. But no matter how much money I had or owed at any given time, I was devoted to helping others in need. My friends knew this, especially one girlfriend who was going through a terrible divorce. She was highly emotional, was strapped for cash, and needed help with her children. I offered to babysit her five kids, brought her groceries, and made myself available on the phone and in person to make her feel better. This went on for some time, and I started to feel exhausted.

Then one day I was horribly ill, yet she kept calling me. I texted her that I was sick in bed, and she responded that she had an emergency and needed to speak to me urgently. I was so worried that I picked up the phone on the next ring, and she immediately asked to borrow $2,000 for attorney fees. I whispered through my raspy voice that I didn't have it, but she pleaded with me, asking if she could charge it to my credit card.

My immune system was already so low that I started shaking and sweating. My entire body told me to say no, but I couldn't speak my truth. She kept begging until I finally caved and agreed to lend her the funds, explaining that I didn't really have any extra resources at that time, and she would have to pay it back. She said yes, and although I wanted to believe she would honor this commitment, I had a sinking feeling in my heart that the money was gone. Once the law firm processed the credit-card payment, my "friend" and I never spoke again.

As much as I wanted to blame her for leaving me with a $2,000 bill and treating me poorly, I was angrier at myself for allowing her to use (or abuse) me. I complained to others and beat myself up about it—but that just depleted my energy even further. I tried calling her and sending her e-mails, but got no response. Nothing good was coming out of playing this same tape over and over, wondering what if I had done this or wishing I had said that. She eventually moved to another part of the country, but I still found myself wasting emotional currency by resenting her and her act of betrayal.

While processing my anger and shame, I had to admit this kind of thing kept happening to me—being taken advantage of, unable to speak up—and I wanted it to stop. It wasn't even so much about the money; I was more concerned about why I didn't trust my gut and why I kept doing things that ended up hurting me. I yearned to uncover what was going on so I could stop leaving myself open to be disrespected or abused in the future. I desperately wanted to stop this cycle once and for all, but for the life of me, I couldn't figure out what I needed to do.

The Origin of the Loops

My solution was to go on an inward journey. I've always kept a personal journal, but in 2011, I wrote all the time, trying to sort out my feelings and my life. I meditated daily. I enrolled in the part-time graduate program at John F. Kennedy University and intensely studied the relationship between my mind and my behaviors.

I realized that my life was made up of two main recurring themes: times when I was deeply stuck in fear, and then other times when I was immersed in gratitude. My life consisted of many different cycles of intense lack, chaos, and fear . . . yet at times I experienced moments of intense gratitude.

While journaling during this period, I noticed that I was also doodling circles and loops along with my writing. Then in 2012, I made a breakthrough. While overanalyzing the loan incident in my journal yet another time, questioning my stupidity and my inability to stand up for myself, I again started drawing loops. I felt I was going around and around in a vicious cycle, and I wanted to understand what was causing me to make the decisions that I did.

I saw then that I was stuck in a loop of fear. My fear of not being enough made me feel anxious, which led me to make poor choices, and sure enough, the outcome was negative. That's when I first drew the Scarcity Loop. It felt so right. I had finally figured out what was going on with me!

A month later, we celebrated my daughter's ninth birthday. I felt so much gratitude that I had to write about it at the end of that glorious day, thanking God for blessing me with such a perfect and loving child. I thanked him for bringing this divine being into this world healthy, happy, and beautiful.

When I am in that state of deep gratitude, I experience such peace of mind that I'm able to see things much more clearly. From that vantage point and awareness, I'm able to make much better choices in all areas of my life. That's when I first drew the

Abundance Loop, and I got chills. I immediately glimpsed a better way to live, and I wanted to live in abundance and gratitude more than anything.

A few days after that, I learned I was pregnant with my third child and felt deeply grateful that my new husband, Chris, and I were going to have a baby together. After celebrating over lunch, I flew to Denver, Colorado, to attend the Hay House Writer's Workshop, feeling abundant. I was sleeping in a hotel when a deep, prolonged whirring noise followed by a short, high-pitched braking of a railcar woke me up. I grabbed my journal and immediately wrote *Balance*.

That single word erupted into a cascade of ideas and a long writing session about juxtaposing opposites: scarcity and abundance, fear and gratitude, inner and outer, financial and spiritual, yin and yang . . . all reflecting balance. I would not have craved freedom so much had I not felt enslaved. I would not have sought peace and understanding had I not suffered through turmoil and confusion. I could not have developed the Abundance Loop without understanding the Scarcity Loop.

I am now excited to share the power of these loops with you. Let's begin with the Scarcity Loop, since we can't get far without understanding the root of our fears.

Stuck in Scarcity

This theory and the techniques related to it are based on finding balance between scarcity and abundance. Scarcity is a state of mind, a loop of negative thoughts rooted in fear. It stalks all of us: not only do we fear not having enough, but we also fear not being enough. We may even fear our own perfectly Divine Self.

Fear causes anxiety, and we don't like how it makes us feel. We take action to suppress the sense that something's not quite right. Whether we prefer shopping, eating, drinking, smoking, or fighting, our "drug of choice" numbs our physical or emotional pain and the nagging we feel inside. We find temporary relief and mistake it for happiness. But the absence of pain doesn't equal joy.

These fear-based thoughts can blur our ability to make sound choices. Poor choices ultimately lead to negative outcomes, which generate more fear . . . and around and around it goes. We get trapped in the Scarcity Loop.

Many of us, myself included, see this loop operating in various aspects of our lives: finances, career, relationships, health, family, community, and so on. My decision to lend the money to my friend is reflected in the Scarcity Loop. I felt anxious about making her feel bad, and I valued her feelings more than I valued my own. Although I knew I should say no, I agreed to call her attorney with my credit-card information. As soon as the charges went through, I recognized that I would suffer the consequences of not listening to my inner voice and instead succumbing to someone else's voice.

Chances are, many of your past choices were also rooted in fear. As you go through this book, you will be asked to take the time to challenge your beliefs about what is possible and see that you have what it takes right now to create the life you want.

Although we all want to break out of the Scarcity Loop, it's not a onetime event. I sure wish it was, but the truth is that moving through scarcity and into abundance is a constantly evolving process. The key is to not get stuck in scarcity; learn the things to watch for and quickly check yourself on that old thinking. As you will find out, when you cultivate awareness and gratitude on a consistent basis, you will more easily be able to loosen fear's grip on you and shift into the Abundance Loop more often and stay there longer. The tools are all here, including this checklist about how to recognize the signs of scarcity in your life.

EXERCISE:
Are You Suffering from Symptoms of Scarcity?

Surely you don't want to live the majority of your life in scarcity. An important part of getting out of scarcity is recognizing you are in it. Here are some of the common signs that you or someone you love might be suffering from scarcity and stuck in a pattern of behavior that needs to change.

- **Hoarding.** Do you impulsively shop and collect yet another item that takes up more space—space that you probably don't have? As you find peace with yourself, it is easier to curb the shopping addiction.

- **Attachment to Old Possessions.** Do you hang on stubbornly to threadbare or unworn clothing and barely used equipment? Time to let go of what no longer serves you and make space for what does.

- **Hanging Out with Exhausting People.** Do you spend too much time with people who exhaust you and make you feel bad about yourself? Time to wean yourself off these so-called friends and find a more personally supportive group.

- **Overworking.** Do you work extremely long hours on a regular basis at the expense of time with your family or taking care of your health? Time to reassess what's truly important to you.

- **Complaining.** Do you often voice your dissatisfaction about what you lack, what didn't go right, and what bothers you? This is a habit you can change once you're aware of it and reset your life for fulfillment.

- **Wasting Time.** Do you get easily distracted by texts, e-mails, housework, or other nonessential activities? Channel your time and energy into what you actually want to manifest.

- **Clutter.** Do you live in chaos and complain about not being able to find anything? Reclaim your power over your stuff and make space that you truly appreciate.

- **Lack of Follow-through.** When opportunities come your way, do you neglect to follow up and instead come up with excuses? This also manifests as starting projects but not seeing them through to completion.

- **Inability to Say No.** Whether it's regarding food, drugs, sex, or alcohol, do you lack self-control and allow your addictions to get the best of you? And do you always want to please others, and therefore find yourself just unable to say no to anybody, regardless of what is asked of you?

- **Depriving Yourself.** Do you deprive yourself of small pleasures in your life, such as an ice-cream cone on a hot day? Even if you're feeling poor, when you deny yourself every pleasurable thing, it doesn't help you save more money; it just reinforces your scarcity mind-set.

This is just a checklist for you to become aware of some of the ways in which scarcity might be manifesting in your daily life. Fortunately, this book covers these and many more signs of scarcity and shares different ways to rise above it. One of the first is getting a handle on the underlying fears that are running your life.

What Are You Afraid Of?

At this point, we know that the Scarcity Loop is rooted in fear. We all experience this primal emotion throughout our lives, and we don't need to suppress or deny it out of shame. Yet, we do. Fear, which is an organic animal emotion, evolved to protect us from dangers in our environment.

When our early ancestors felt threatened, they instinctively took self-protective action to increase their chances of survival. Those who didn't notice or ignored danger signals died. While many of the perils faced by our ancestors no longer exist in modern, civilized life, our brains continue to react to perceived dangers by triggering fear *even when our survival is not actually at risk.* We inherited this natural bias toward fear. We can't eliminate it, nor would we want to, for fear can motivate us and push us to new heights.

Fear is a particularly powerful emotion, and it drives our behaviors, whether we are conscious of it or not. When we fall short of "enough," we feel like crap and we end up doing just about anything to alleviate this discomfort.

We often turn to other vices to avoid dealing with that awful belief that we're not enough. Even when we channel the energy of fear into something positive such as work, exercise, or friends, we can get addicted to the high that comes from temporarily soothing our fear of inadequacy and become overly attached to our job, sport, or relationships. This is also true of our attachment to money . . . *and the lack of money.*

I've seen many people let money slip through their fingers for numerous reasons. Some cling to their poverty as much as others cling to their wealth. Fear perpetuates the attachment to poverty and to wealth. It is this desperate grasping that blocks abundance from flowing into your life.

People often dream of the good life, and why shouldn't you also follow your dreams? You can own a home, be able to afford nice meals and clothes, have access to reliable health care, have fun with friends and family, and do things that bring you joy. You say you want it all, but something holds you back from attaining your heart's desire. Instead of facing things head-on, you moan about your job, your bills, the economy, unemployment, the housing market, taxes, the rising cost of food and child care, and all the other things that you think are thwarting your plans.

It is by becoming aware of your fears and the stories you spin around them that you can begin to let them go so you can move through life with ease. As you proceed through the steps, answer the questions I pose, and practice the exercises, you will learn how to break down your fears and eventually accept the amazing wealth you hold inside and let it flow out and into this world.

Childhood Fears and Ego

Where do you suppose your unreasonable fears originated in the first place? All of us want to feel safe and secure. As a young child, you experienced moments when your needs were not completely met, and that threatened your sense of security. Even the "best" caretaker or parent is not always attuned to every physical and emotional need of a child. In some ways this is healthy, because the child is then forced to grow up and learn to take care of him- or herself. Along the way, however, the child will feel anxious, and will develop what psychologists call a "defended self" in order to cope. This defended self is a distorted view of who you really are, and it forms part of your ego.

Here's how this scenario likely played out: Maybe one day you innocently ran to tell your mom about a new freckle you just discovered. Instead of sharing your enthusiasm, she rebuked you for interrupting her phone conversation. Because you were a child, your reasoning skills hadn't yet developed enough to understand that, although she loved you, you hadn't picked a good moment to express your excitement. Instead, you interpreted her irritated tone and annoyed look to mean that not only did your freckle not matter—*you* didn't matter. In that moment, your impressionable mind unconsciously absorbed the belief "I am not worthy enough for Mom to pay attention to me." From then on, this painful experience and others like it became indelibly imprinted in your mind, especially in relation to those things that happened often in your life.

Then as you grew up, those early impressions or "imprints" stayed with you. Even today, your fear of not being enough may continue to fuel your ambitions to climb a corporate ladder. Maybe each raise and promotion validates your self-worth but is never quite enough to make you feel that you have what you need. Perhaps this makes you want to work even harder, and you catapult yourself into your job: working late hours and weekends, often at the expense of connecting with your friends and family, and adversely affecting your physical and mental health.

We all experience a version of this, and many of us attach ourselves to a select few "hurts" that we tend to talk about over and over, repeating them to ourselves and to our friends, partners, therapists, and whoever else might be willing to listen. The replays of these stories keep our fear-based memories alive and our egos strong.

Stress tends to make things even worse. When stress triggers your fear of not being enough, you may then react irrationally and blame others for "hurting" you, reinforcing your sense of abandonment and neglect. Whether these threats are real or imagined, many of us have developed armor plating to protect our fragile egos and selves. Defense mechanisms such as shutting down, getting angry, and redirecting energy may have helped you adjust to a childhood trauma, but if these mechanisms continue to be overused as you proceed through your life, they can create thick walls that form a psychological fortress. And regrettably, your true and Divine Self can become imprisoned within it. The defense that served you well as a child hinders you as an adult.

Fear of Not Enough

Two main fears stand out here: the fear of not having enough and the fear of not being enough. The first one is on the surface and easier to see, but beneath the fear of not having enough lurks the invisible one—the fear of not *being* enough.

Our fast-paced, consumer-oriented culture thrives on our fears and desires. Mass media and peer pressure tantalize us with the good life—the more money, food, sex, beauty, love, and fun we get, the happier we will be. You probably recognize yourself in some version of this common desire: *I want more. I need more money so I can be happy.* Modern society tells us that by getting rich, we can have all the stuff we want. *Then* we will be happy!

But the problem doesn't lie with power, money, or beauty, nor with working hard to earn more or paying attention to your physical appearance. In fact, I appreciate these values and applaud efforts to manifest them. The problem lies with our underlying assumptions. We assume that wealth exists outside us and that we do not have enough.

Let's take a simple example. Perhaps you just saw this season's "must-have" fashion trend, so you click online or run out to buy the latest boots and a purse to match. You rationalize the surge of guilt by telling yourself that you work hard and you deserve these things. You relish your new look and feel excited when friends and co-workers compliment you.

Maybe you've found happiness for the moment—at least until next season's collection shows up. When it does, you'll soon feel inadequate again. Old fears of not having enough—of not *being* enough—are quite likely to resurface. Not to worry, though—there's a way out. And it starts from the inside.

Reclaiming Your Power from Your Ego

We have already established that as an infant and young child, you didn't get everything you wanted. Sometimes, you felt deprived of *things,* other times, of touch, comfort, love, food, or friends; and this left you feeling that "something is wrong." You assumed something was wrong with *you.* Unconsciously, you felt threatened. Your survival was at stake. Your young mind instinctively reacted defensively, trying to protect your vulnerable little body, and you developed a sense of "I" and "me." Your ego came into being.

Your ego evolved to serve you, but it thinks it *is* you, and tries to run the show. It's a master of irony: The ego does everything it can to avoid fear—yet, as a defense mechanism, it actually creates the reality you fear most.

Here's how it works. Let's say you fear abandonment and develop a hard outer shell to protect you from ever getting hurt. You use anger as a weapon of choice to protect your vulnerable self. Yet this armor keeps others away. People can't truly connect with you and they don't appreciate getting yelled at, so they leave you. How useful, then, is such armor? Designed to protect you, your ego defenses work so well that they resulted in the abandonment you feared the most in the first place. You end up in a Scarcity Loop where you manifested the very outcomes you tried to avoid, creating a self-fulfilling prophecy.

Let's look at another example. Let's say you fear that you do not matter. You feel anxious about it, so you do everything you can to prove to others that you do indeed matter. But the harder you try, the less they appreciate your efforts, which triggers your fear of not mattering—and around you go. The following illustration shows this Scarcity Loop in action, one that I unconsciously lived for many years.

The process of uncovering your underlying fears is not an easy one. It takes deep introspection and might bring up uncomfortable emotions, but it's an invaluable exercise. I've written out directions below and some questions to help you first identify your fears and then start to release them.

EXERCISE:
Letting Go of Your Fears

It's now your turn to draw one of your own Scarcity Loops and uncover what is going on. I know it doesn't sound like fun. Most people don't actively go looking to dig up their crap, but identifying your fears is a critical step in breaking free of scarcity. Start by taking a deep breath. Imagine you are just watching a movie of your life unfold. Sit back and try to calmly observe what comes up.

Take out your journal and a pen, or open a fresh document on your laptop. Try to answer the following questions. There is no right or wrong answer, no good or bad; whatever images or words come up are exactly what is meant to come up.

Just jot down whatever unfolds in your mind without second-guessing it or passing judgment.

Allow yourself to feel each emotion that comes up. You will start by observing your external reality and then move inward to observe your internal workings. I offer a couple different questions to help you pinpoint the key elements of your Scarcity Loop.

Undesirable Outcomes:

- What situation in your life brings you a lot of stress?

- What negative outcome seems to keep recurring?

Poor Choices:

- What choice did you make that resulted in this outcome?

- What actions did you take or fail to take?

Emotions:

- How were you feeling before you took that action?

- What thoughts were running through your head?

- What did you feel? What did you *not* want to feel?

Fear:

- What were you afraid of?

- What is the deeper fear beneath that?

Once you answer these questions, draw your own Scarcity Loop, starting with your fear on top. Continue clockwise and write your emotion at 3 o'clock on the circle, your choice at the bottom of the circle, and the undesirable result at 9 o'clock. Wow. Take a deep breath and process what may have just come up for you. Reflect on how often this pattern shows up in your life. Repeat the process several times if you wish, to bring up your second-most-stressful thing, your third, and more if you feel there is more.

Now that you have identified your fears and are starting to understand them, it's time to rewrite your script. Below is a list of examples of how you can shift your fear-based script into one that delivers freedom.

So whenever you catch yourself saying the usual fear-based statements in Column 1 below, try replacing that thought with the statement across from it in Column 2. Repeat the new statement at least ten times with conviction in your voice, and keep repeating it until you start to feel the freedom of this new thinking at your core. As you repeat your new freedom script, you will find that in time, your fears will subside, and abundant thinking will become a new mental habit. Another great overall statement to repeat to yourself is: "I am taking charge of my fears and stepping into my abundance!"

Recognize your old fear-based script	Replace with your new freedom-based script
I can't do it.	I can do whatever I set my mind to.
I can't afford to get what I want.	I can make different choices to get what I want.
I have no control over my life or what others do to me.	I have full control over how I approach life and how I respond to others.
I am not worthy enough unless I . . .	I am enough right now.

Be aware that you may have to go through this process a few more times, when any other fears arise or in the event that you find yourself stuck in another pesky Scarcity Loop. And remember, this is just one technique, and there are many more in this book that will also help you replace those old feelings of fear with concrete, positive beliefs and actions. Your loop is about to change, and I'm so happy for you.

Moving from Fear to Gratitude

This whole book is about the process of moving from scarcity to abundance. It was so exciting when the concept of the Abundance Loop first appeared to me.

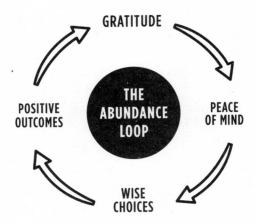

As indicated in the sketch, the Abundance Loop begins with gratitude. When you take the time to appreciate what you have, you focus on what is present, not absent. You appreciate the abundance you behold instead of fretting about what's lacking. Whether this lack is perceived or real, concentrating on "not having enough" tethers you to scarcity. In contrast, cultivating gratitude brings you peace of mind. When your mind is calm, you make better choices, choices that are more likely to give rise to positive outcomes. As good things start to happen, and your actions yield results you want, suddenly you have more reasons to give thanks . . . and around you go.

So now, you can see how the Abundance Loop can bolster your financial and emotional well-being. But how can you shift from the Scarcity Loop to the Abundance Loop? Do you want to move from living in fear to living in gratitude? You can, and that part of the process begins with awareness, a topic we'll talk about in more detail in Step 2.

You Always Have a Choice

As you can see, choices lie at the heart of both the Scarcity Loop and the Abundance Loop. Whether you choose to break free from scarcity or not is up to you. You have deliberate control over what you do at any given moment. Even choosing to believe that you have no choice is a choice. You can stay in a job you hate and complain about not having a choice, but the fact is, *you always have a choice.*

If you are truly dissatisfied about something in your life, I encourage you to make a conscious choice to change. We will dive deeper into this topic in Step 6: Commit to Conscious Action.

The concepts of awareness and gratitude are so integral to this process of making the conscious choice to live in the Abundance Loop that I have made a point to cover these two ideas in detail in Step 2 and Step 3, respectively. As you follow along with the stories, questions, and exercises in those steps, you will soon find yourself inhabiting a whole new perspective and starting to enjoy a new, more abundant existence. To jump-start your thinking, I'd like to tell you about how a friend and I used these principles to support each other in coming to terms with our own fears.

Josie's Flow into Abundance

A high-functioning go-getter, my friend Josie still felt stuck in the Scarcity Loop. She had achieved success in her career, quickly rising through the ranks at a Fortune 500 company, where she worked long, intense hours both at the office and at home. To treat herself, she went on shopping binges and never blinked at the prices. She ate out every night or grabbed takeout, drank multiple shots of espresso and cans of Diet Coke throughout the day, and ended every night with a couple of cocktails.

Stunning, sexy, and smart, Josie attracted many men, but she always came up with creative excuses to end those relationships. Yet the real reason she could not commit to any of them over the long term was because she was afraid of turning out like her mother. Her mother was financially and emotionally dependent on a man who had married her but over time lost respect for her and eventually left her.

The stress of Josie's workaholic lifestyle eventually took a toll on her physical and financial health, and she silently suffered from an autoimmune disease. Josie was emotional as she finally opened up to me about her pain, sharing that the inflammation would get so bad sometimes that she could barely clasp her hands or even walk.

Josie finally realized that if she didn't seek help, she could die. She began by working with a nutritionist to change her diet and reduce her caffeine and alcohol consumption. The changes were so effective that she then tackled other aspects of her life with the guidance of a professional therapist. She was shocked when she stepped back and added up all the hours she was working and all the money she was spending on stuff she didn't really need. But the worst was the energy drain she experienced in her efforts to keep up her image, to feel good about herself and impress others. Her perfect persona won validation and praise in the corporate world, but now she was petrified that this disease might get the best of her, exposing her ugliness.

I was heartbroken to hear that she thought of herself as less than amazing inside and out. Not only was she beautiful with a fantastic personality, but she was also super fun to be with; and despite her efforts to hide it, she had a huge heart. When I listed all her wonderful qualities, she started to glow. I told her that I understood her frenetic pace because I too worked hard to gain approval and needed external validation of my own worth.

Although we were very different people in many ways, Josie and I shared the same root fear as everyone else: We didn't feel that we could express our true selves because we didn't believe we were enough. In sharing our stories, we both found healing. As we got stronger, we were able to grow into our authentic selves, support each other, and find peace and joy.

The lesson I took from my experience with Josie was that it is our fears (or rather, our stories about our fears) that hinder us from experiencing real abundance. When you are willing to face your deepest fears, the ones that are standing in your way, you will open up to what you truly want and deserve: an abundant life.

Finding Your Own Divinity

Writing this book and setting up the engine to promote my message has taken significant time, money, and a whole lot of energy! So why do I bother? It's simple: *because you are worth it.* You are a divine being with a divine purpose. And I know how hard it is to actualize your full divine potential while operating in a Scarcity Loop, because I have been there.

Needless to say, there are a lot of problems in this world. But collectively, if we could shift beyond our egos and embody our true, authentic, divine essence, we would make better decisions that would create a healthier and more sustainable world.

Think about it. By aligning with your abundant and Divine Self, you wouldn't need to consume as much as you usually do. You would make better choices about what to do with your money, time, and energy. You have enormous energy, but it's not limitless.

The more conscious you become of how you spend your physical, mental, emotional, and spiritual energy, the more you can give your best to yourself, to others, and to the world.

If you aren't sure what I mean when I refer to you and your "Divine Self," please know that I'm not referencing any one divinity, religion, or God in particular. Feel free to replace the words *God* and *Divine Self* with whatever, to you, means your highest self, your essence, your authentic nature, your true self, your soul, or your own Universal Truth. Essentially, choose whatever term connotes something greater than you that you trust and that you can surrender to.

So even though I happened to grow up as a Christian and I do believe in God, I want to emphasize that it isn't my intention to influence your religious or spiritual belief system; rather, I just encourage you to visualize yourself as more than who you think you are, and definitely more than who you present yourself to be in the world.

Balancing Money and Spirit

At this point you might be wondering: *Why in the world is a financial advisor writing a spiritual self-help book instead of focusing only on the financial how-to techniques?* Throughout my career, I have worked with hundreds of men and women and given numerous seminars. I absolutely love speaking to people either individually or in large audiences and empowering them to achieve their financial dreams. However, as time went by, I saw that most needed more than investment education and access to financial tools. They needed assurance and self-confidence that they could expand their vision about what is possible and truly transform their lives.

The key issue I have seen repeatedly in adults of all ages, from their 20s to their 80s, high-school dropouts and those with Ph.D.'s alike—people on Wall Street and on Main Street, from all backgrounds, cultures, and religions—boils down to one common core belief. You guessed it . . . it is that is that they are not enough.

I knew then if I really wanted to influence people and help them experience peace and fulfillment, I needed to go beyond dollars and cents. I needed to go beyond data, logic, flowcharts, analysis, and portfolio reviews. I could design the most elegant financial plan, but the report might just sit in a filing cabinet and never be implemented. I needed to tackle the real crux of their problem, which is their mind-set.

Living in the Abundance Loop, I notice now how I show up in the world differently. I've learned to slow down and accept that whatever I am doing, I am enough. By accepting myself and giving thanks for all that I am, I feel at peace. With the deep knowing that I am enough and I have enough, I'm able to conserve my precious resources; and I can consciously allocate my time, money, and energy in a balanced manner.

For example, I used to serve on the board of a nonprofit. Although I loved the organization and its mission, balancing it while I was working and raising young children, and while going to school and trying to write a book, was just too much. I recognized that I was adding enough value to this world by being present in my role as mother to my kids and financial advisor to my clients.

I had come so far from the time when I was stuck in the Scarcity Loop as I described at the beginning of this chapter. Had I recognized that I was adding enough value to my "friend" by emotionally supporting her through her divorce and by physically showing up to help her family, I would not have let her take financial advantage of me as well. But, eventually, I broke the cycle of not speaking up, and I did so by fully accepting the belief that *I am enough.*

With this belief in my heart, I found that I was able to cordially resign from the nonprofit board that was no longer my biggest priority. I felt at peace about the decision and felt great about respecting my current needs enough to put them before the needs of any organization. I now have more energy and time to devote to my health, my family, my wealth-management practice, and my writing. And I am thrilled to be writing next about two of my favorite topics: building awareness and reframing beliefs.

Key Messages about Choosing to Break Free from Scarcity

- Scarcity stems from fear of not *having* enough and fear of not *being* enough.

- Fear is a natural emotion, but we unconsciously let it dominate our lives by resisting it.

- Living in the Abundance Loop means letting go of the attachments that keep you stuck in scarcity.

- Awareness of your fears opens the pathway to abundance.

STEP 2

Challenge Your Beliefs and Raise Your Awareness

You are the boss of your own life. However, it's hard to hear the boss if you're busy listening to everyone else. We all have looming voices in our heads, a chorus of different people who have influenced us throughout life, speaking to us—sometimes shouting—through the protective layers of our ego.

This inner dialogue can be as simple as *I shouldn't have bought those shoes. I can't afford them. But they look so cute, and my friends will be so jealous.* This is soon followed by the next part of the inner script: *Why do you care what they think? Stop wasting money.* Or maybe you've heard this kind of inner talk: *What should I make for dinner? I hope my son's science project isn't due this week since work is crazy. Oh, I can't forget to call my aunt back.* And then there is the standard favorite: *Wow, I really need to exercise more,* or *I've got to save more,* or *I've got to make more money.*

Sounds chaotic, doesn't it? But this kind of chatter goes on every waking hour of our days. Researchers have been trying to figure out for years just how many thoughts the average person has in a day, giving estimates that range anywhere from 7,000 to 70,000 thoughts a day. They appear so fast that no one can really count them! Shockingly, various online research sources indicate that the average person thinks positive thoughts only about 30 percent of the time, meaning that negative thoughts fill our heads about 70 percent of the time. Negative thoughts are a symptom of anxiety, and, unfortunately, anxiety can perpetuate more bad thoughts, entrapping you in the Scarcity Loop.

I know that your inner script will be different from the one about shoes, dinner, and working out, but one thing is certain: You have *some version* of a script running through your head, morning, noon, and night. If you don't believe me, just take 15 minutes to sit quietly and observe the incessant chatter of your "monkey mind." As you go through this Step, I will explain more about this process and provide a number of practical skills that will help you bring down the level of chatter and get rid of the negative self-talk that is holding you back from abundance.

Busy, Busy, Busy

Have you ever wondered where all that negative self-talk comes from anyway? Well, that would be your "inner critic." We all have one. Your inner critic carries the loudest and most powerful voice of them all, judging you sharply about everything you do. This critic draws on an amalgamation of past messages from your parents and other influencers, and the sound feels harsh and confines you within a prison of scarcity, fear, and self-loathing. Do judgments like these sound familiar?

- "Why did you do that?"

- "You're so stupid!"

- "You don't make enough money."

- "Can't you do anything right?"

So with all this going through your head, you might say that you want peace and quiet, that you want to calm the chorus and your inner critic, *but what are your actions saying?* What message are you sending when you leave your phone on during dinner, ready to pick up on the first ring? Or when you spend your weekends running as many errands as possible instead of resting or enjoying family time? What about your habit of packing your social calendar so tight that you often double-book friends and events because you are just so busy and don't want to let anyone down?

All these busy, busy, busy actions may make you *feel* that you're in control, but in actuality, you are inviting even more distractions and chaos into your life. You'd like to believe you are adding value to the world with all that running around, but this whirlwind of activity is not just unnecessary; it's compromising your physical, mental, and financial well-being.

Fortunately, there are two practical and powerful ways to get a better handle on your life and unlock your divine abundance. The first is to harness the power of your breath, which can significantly heighten your awareness. I will begin by reintroducing you to your own breathing—the breath of life—something I suspect you may have been ignoring for quite some time. The second part is to understand how your mind works and how to take control of your own thoughts.

Why would I ask you to breathe? Wouldn't you be doing that anyway, every day, 24/7? Yes, of course. But I want you to learn that you can use your breath to practice quieting your mind and observing your thought patterns. As you do so, you'll develop the awareness that you are not your thoughts. This bears repeating, especially if it's a new concept to you. This is a critical fact to understand, so please repeat it along with me, out loud: "I am *not* my thoughts."

Once this dawns on you, suddenly you will see that your inner critic may not actually be speaking the truth. You can realize that you have a choice to either accept or reject what your inner critic is saying. You can choose to let go of this false and destructive belief system that has been masking your true and Divine Self. It works because when you see something as separate from you, you can make a choice whether to continue to hold on to it or not. How incredibly liberating!

EXERCISE:
Introducing the Breath of Life

The practice of quieting your mind begins with noticing your breath and learning how to direct it in a conscious way so that you can open up to a host of good things to come. Here's a technique to start getting in touch with your breathing so you can use it to transform your life.

First, take a moment and just sit quietly in a comfortable position (on a chair, on the floor, or wherever you can feel both relaxed and alert). Now, _do nothing,_ except simply notice that you are breathing. Spend a few minutes. Notice how it feels.

Isn't it remarkable that you don't have to _remember_ to breathe? Your body does it naturally.

Now, pay attention to the beating of your heart. Do you notice anything different about your breathing versus your beating heart? Of all of the body's automatic processes, breathing is unique because it responds to _conscious attention_ in ways our other automatic functions do not (or, at least, rarely do without lengthy and dedicated biofeedback practice).

Breathing happens all by itself, yet we can also consciously control it. This simple fact is one reason why focusing attention on our breath helps us become aware of the deep connection between mind and body—one of the main benefits of meditation.

Now try this next step. Sit quietly. Slowly inhale through your nose. Hold your breath for about five seconds. Then slowly exhale through your mouth (even make an audible sigh as you release your breath). Breathe in. Breathe out. You naturally perform this simple act many times a minute, supplying body and mind with energy vital for the process of life.

Now, take notice of how just focusing on your breath tends to draw you into the present moment. You shift away from worrying about what happened yesterday or what will happen tomorrow. Instead, you focus on what is occurring right now. You listen to the inhalation and exhalation of your breath, and observe your stomach and chest rise and fall. You become attuned to your own rhythms.

When you do this, don't try to change or suppress your thoughts, because that will just give them more fuel and power. Instead, learn to *just notice them.* This is where conscious choice comes in—not to *change* your thoughts, but to *choose* to simply observe your thoughts as they come and go (which they do naturally). Choosing to let go of your thoughts (to merely witness them) is just like choosing to observe breathing. In both cases, you focus conscious attention on processes that usually happen unconsciously.

Watching your breathing and clearing your mind in this way has been called many things, including practicing mindfulness, doing meditation, or witnessing, among others. With some conscious practice over time, you become aware that you are neither your body nor your thoughts. You *have* a body and you *have* thoughts—but "you" are the *awareness* of what happens in your body and your mind.

When you focus on your breath, you simply observe what is going on, including your thoughts. As challenging as it is, you can alter your thought patterns just as you can alter your breathing patterns—through *conscious choice.*

Next, you will realize that you always have three options:

1. To let your breathing happen automatically and
    unconsciously;

2. To focus awareness on, and simply observe, this natural
    process; or

3. To consciously choose to control the flow of your breath.

Experimenting with these options during the practice of mindfulness helps you realize that the process of breathing is much like the process of thinking. Both come and go, rise and fall, automatically without you doing anything; yet both also respond to conscious intervention.

The Many Benefits of a Mindfulness Practice

So now you know that practicing mindfulness quiets the mind and opens you to fully experience the present—including all your thoughts and sensations. It is a practical and easy way to reconnect to the depths of your being and to all of life. It brings you into the here and now, heightening your senses so you can consciously embrace the moment through sight, sound, smell, taste, and touch. Mindfulness illuminates the power inherent in each moment, where you connect with new possibilities.

For centuries, people across many religions have taken time to be in silence and focus attention on prayer—in stillness or in action. Mindfulness is a way to bring awareness and intention to what you are doing and *being* in the present moment—to whatever is going on.

For example, you can eat mindfully, savoring the flavors and textures of the food; you can walk or run mindfully, feeling the support of the ground beneath your feet; and you can dialogue mindfully, paying attention to your own emotions, thoughts, and bodily sensations, while being fully present to others. You can even balance your checkbook and at the same time notice how you react in both mind and body to whatever the numbers reveal about your financial status and your relationship to money. In all cases, mindfulness is about allowing yourself the freedom to just be who you are and experience what is.

When you're quiet, your ego defenses melt away, revealing your authentic self. Things become clearer. You finally have clarity about who you are, what you want, and even how to get it. When you quiet the internalized voices of others, you more clearly hear your own wisdom, sometimes called your Higher Self. Deep down, you have all the answers to your questions. You know what's best for you, but it's hard to hear and trust your inner voice because you confuse it with your inner critic.

So how can you tell the difference between your inner voice and your inner critic? The inner voice sounds calm, helpful, and enlightening. Upon hearing it, you relax and open up and expand your heart. Your inner voice revitalizes you and brings a smile to your face. With peace of mind, you feel empowered. Your inner critic does just the opposite. Harsh and destructive, your inner judge prevents you from living your Divine Self. You feel belittled, tightly wound, and disempowered. Your heart beats faster, your chest and jaw tighten, your breath shallows, and worry and anger lines set more prominently.

You may tend to depend on others for advice and guidance because you've lost the connection to who you truly are. I agree that at times, others can see us more clearly than we see ourselves. However, you can feel overwhelmed and at a loss when confronted with too many options, too many people, whether in reality or in your head, telling you contradictory things. This is also true when you are seeking financial advice; you can find dozens of people to give you advice and not all of it will agree. It can become hugely confusing and frustrating.

However, while we're sitting (or walking) in silence, answers come naturally to each of us, of their own accord, rising up from the inherent wisdom of our own body and mind, formed over millions of years of evolution. Being quiet allows us to access our innate power and wisdom.

EXERCISE:
Starting to Quiet Your Mind

Now that you've tried working with your breath and you understand how valuable it can be to get control of your thoughts, it's time to learn how to quiet your mind. Some people may be able to do so just by looking out their window at tree branches waving in the wind. Others calm themselves in prayer. This basic exercise will take you through one way to practice mindfulness. Another meditation is at the end of this step, and it focuses more on your abundant self. As you practice these kinds of exercises, you will develop the best techniques for you.

1. You will need between five minutes to half an hour a day to do this important exercise. I recommend you commit to doing it every day for a week, for however long you think best each day, in order to get started.

2. First sit or lie down in a quiet, private place where you will not be disturbed by another person.

3. Close your eyes if you feel comfortable doing so and focus on the natural rhythm of your breathing. Gauge your level of tension simply by listening to and feeling your breath. As you inhale the air around you and exhale the used-up air within you, try to connect to your inner world.

4. As you reach a calm and tranquil place inside yourself, you become aware of the difference between the chorus of voices that come from other people and outside pressures, and the true voice of your own Divine Self.

5. As you sit quietly, gradually let your ego defenses melt away. Visualize that you are turning down the volume knob on all the "monkey mind" chatter in your head. Imagine space opening up for your authentic self to emerge. Breathe into that space. Every time you practice mindfulness in any way that is comfortable for you, you can enjoy a dialogue with your authentic inner self and a feeling of greater clarity. Remember, your Divine Self can also be called by other names, such as your Higher Self, your inner wisdom, your intuition, or simply your gut. Use whatever wording feels right. You know what's best for you.

6. When your mindfulness-practice time is up, begin to gradually return to your regular breathing and open your eyes if you had them closed. Be grateful for the experience. You may want to write down some important ideas or bits of advice that came to you during this practice.

Listening to Your Inner Wisdom

As you continue to develop your ability to understand and listen to your Divine Self, you will find that you quite naturally begin to move from the Scarcity Loop toward the Abundance Loop. You will discover that you feel calmer, even when you are under pressure. Your daily questions will be answered naturally, with your own internal wisdom coming to you of its own accord. You will access your innate power, knowledge, and strength.

Most important of all, you will understand that you are enough. In fact, you are divine! When you accept this truth and ground your thoughts and actions in this truth, you feel abundant in every moment. You will understand that your real wealth is not measured by money, status, or quantity. Abundance can only be measured by how fulfilled and content you are to be you.

With daily practice, you will continually strengthen your beliefs and thought patterns about who you really are. And that's the next part of this step, which is getting rid of your old beliefs and replacing them with new beliefs that serve you better.

Who Do You Believe You Are?

We all hold on to beliefs about who we are and what is possible. Have you ever asked yourself how true these beliefs are? I am astounded and saddened when I hear statements such as these:

- "I'll never be rich."

- "There's never enough."

- "I'm not good enough."

- "I'll never be happy."

These self-limiting beliefs keep you stuck in the Scarcity Loop. When you believe that money is not within your grasp, you get discouraged and give up. Or worse, you may not even try. When the running script in your head is, *I don't have enough to save for the future,* you don't put money away, and, therefore, you lack a nest egg. You create a self-fulfilling prophecy. If we believe something is not in the realm of possibility, we don't bother wasting our energy trying; thus, it doesn't ever become a reality.

I hear many people say they can't afford to quit their jobs. And you know something, they're right. They tell themselves that they can't quit and then spend their full paychecks (and then more on credit) so that they make it harder and harder to ever quit their jobs. People who are dependent on their employers' paychecks are not free. Yes, I know, I recognize that you are probably not free . . . *yet.*

But what if I told you that you could be financially free? Would you believe that you could quit your job, spend your time doing what you love, and still receive an income to pay your bills? Probably not. But ask yourself truthfully: What do you have to lose by changing your belief? What would happen if you started to believe that you could indeed save and that you could actually afford to send your children to college or even retire from a grueling job?

I dare you to believe that you can be financially free and that you can be rich.

I need you to believe it.

Because if you can't even believe it, then taking action toward realizing it may prove futile since it's not always an easy road.

For this to work, you must have the faith and conviction to withstand the many temptations that come your way and not let challenges deter you from achieving your dream. Many people start with the best of intentions to change their habits, but they revert to old ways once the going gets tough. They stay stuck because they haven't moved past their old stories of who they are and what is possible.

To help you get over this very important hurdle, I am going to introduce you to some common self-limiting beliefs that get in the way of living your dreams. You'll see how to let go of some of the fear-based beliefs that have defined your identity and shaped your life up to this point. And you'll learn how to reframe them so you can develop a better attitude and start to take the right actions to reach a whole new financial future.

Self-Limiting Belief #1:
I Don't Have Enough Money

This is an offshoot of the fear of not having enough of any-thing. This fear can easily become the thought *I have to have it now,* which is endemic to the Scarcity Loop, making you feel incomplete without the object of temptation. Let me show you how this looks in the Scarcity Loop:

The obvious way to break this cycle is to stop shopping or squandering money on things you don't need. But for most people, restraining themselves from spending feels like punishment or deprivation. Even if you cut up your credit card, you can't change your habits until you are willing to change the beliefs you have about that situation in the first place.

If you have a scarcity mind-set, then refraining from spending feels like torture, like being on a crash diet over Thanksgiving. My intention is not for you to build wealth at the expense of your happiness. I want you to feel both financially and spiritually fulfilled. This is only possible when you shift your attention away from what you *lack* and focus instead on what you have.

When the running script in your mind is *I have enough,* then you feel more at peace. Even when your ego is tugging at you to acquire more stuff, you feel resolute and empowered so you know that you truly don't need it. You have enough.

The more you can hold off on spending today, the more money you will have available for the future. You can buy a cute pair of boots now or invest that paycheck and generate passive income to buy two pairs later (I'll explain the beauty of passive income a little later on). You will come to understand that the route to financial security is not meant to be laden with guilt and deprivation.

In fact, feelings of guilt and deprivation are symptomatic of the Scarcity Loop. When you feel you don't have enough, you look externally to ease that sense of inadequacy. Although upgrading your wardrobe feels good at the moment, that happiness doesn't last, so you will be tempted to take another dose of "inadequacy relief."

Eventually, you will realize that the long-lasting solution doesn't lie outside of you and it cannot be purchased, won, or earned. You actually have the treasure box inside of you right now, a healthy financial future, and all you need to unlock it is to change your perspective from emphasizing what you lack to taking inventory of what you have. The loop, then, begins not with lack but with gratitude.

New Thinking for Belief #1:
I Am Thankful for My Paychecks

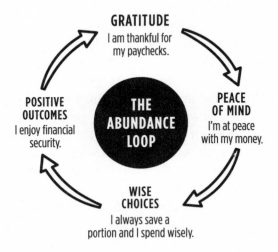

This loop represents a balanced approach to achieving financial security, and it starts with embracing the wealth you already have. No matter how little you feel you have today, if you have the means to purchase and read this book, you have more than you think.

To help you with this, I invite you to visualize something with me. Take a moment to clear your mind and relax. Take a couple of slow, deep breaths. Now I want you to imagine that the company you work for has shut down and you are out of a job. Imagine that every dollar you have in the bank is now gone; and you lost your home, your car, and all your belongings. Then imagine that you lost your partner, your family, your friends, and your pets; and you also had to move from your community. And just for the sake of this exercise, let's keep going and imagine that you have also lost your health, your limbs, your sight, your hearing, your speech, and your ability to read, write, smell, and taste.

How do you feel? How hard would you work to try to get back everything you lost?

Now, shake your head and clear your mind of these tragic thoughts of loss and despair. You haven't lost all these things. Maybe you've lost a few, but you still have an abundance of things to be thankful for, right at your fingertips. Can you believe the abundance you have right now?

Self-Limiting Belief #2:
There's Never Enough Time

When you think about balancing work, children, marriage, friends, church, personal health, and finances, how does that make you feel? If you're like most people, you're probably feeling a bit overwhelmed. When you believe you have to do it all and you have to do it all right now, you feel squeezed for time. This pressure to optimize your time puts you in task mode and you try to juggle it all, very often by attempting to multitask. But studies have shown that only 3 percent of the population can actually multitask efficiently. The rest of us are better off focusing on one task at a time.

This is definitely true in my own family: I know that when my children are with me, they make it clear that they want my full attention. I notice a huge boost in my own level of satisfaction (as well as in my kids' happiness) when I put away my phone, don't worry about my e-mails, and physically get on the floor with them and play. When I'm fully present with them, I can be more engaged and have fun, even if it's just for a few minutes. But when I'm worried about how to respond to a client or what I'm going to write in my next chapter, then I rob my kids—and myself—of that precious moment. I end up feeling guilty for not being a good mom or not being a good professional.

Here's how we can reframe our view of scarcity of time:

New Thinking for Self-Limiting Belief #2:
I Am Thankful for This Moment

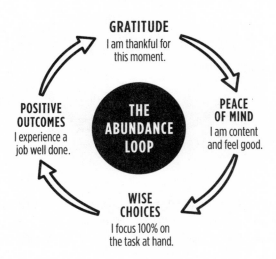

By shifting from fear of not having enough time to gratitude for the time you have, your mind becomes more relaxed and can focus on what's before you. You do the job well and feel good about completing something to the best of your ability. If the task includes another person, then sharing quality time with that person instead of juggling e-mails and texts will result in a stronger relationship. Positive reinforcement supports you to continue operating in the Abundance Loop.

Self-Limiting Belief #3:
Money Is the Root of All Evil

FEAR
Money scares me.

THE SCARCITY LOOP

ANXIETY
I hate money;
it's dirty.

NEGATIVE OUTCOMES
I have no money.

POOR CHOICES
I don't try to earn
a lot and I don't save.

Money is the root of all evil. This is not exactly the wording of the famous phrase in the Bible, but it is the wording that many of us have internalized. The original phrase was more like, "For the love of money is the root of all evil," depending on the translation you might refer to.

What is interesting about this phrase, however you say it, is highlighted in the following story. I had a wonderful conversation with a talented 78-year-old artist named Harold who showed me that it's never too late to change your perception about the rich. He was excited about my speaking on the topic of abundance, and he shared with me what happened when he adjusted his language around rich people relatively late in his life.

Throughout most of his life, Harold was in the habit of calling people with money "filthy rich," and he had little interest in connecting with "those greedy capitalists." But he found that this thinking actually created such a mental separation from people based on how much money they had (or at least appeared to have) that it was damaging his overall energy and vibration around abundance in his own life.

For Harold, *rich* meant having enough resources to devote his time to making beautiful and elaborate collages in his small seaside studio. He felt rich at times but was never "filthy rich." He eventually realized that his disdain for those with a lot of money (his stuck thinking about them) was creating a barrier against those who could afford to purchase his artwork.

When he became aware of this, he asked himself why he should judge others simply because they have the means to afford a more expensive lifestyle. It was then Harold made a conscious effort to let go of his disdain for wealth and stopped calling those other people "filthy rich." He still sees them as privileged, but he widened his perspective to recognize that he enjoys many privileges as well. He has lived and traveled throughout Europe, Asia, and Africa with his family of artists, and together they worked on some amazing and high-profile public art projects. He eventually saw that he is indeed *rich*.

As a result of reflecting about who is rich and what it means to him, Harold now interacts more peacefully with his patrons, taking better care of the money he earns, and feels better about himself.

I share this story because there is value in taking stock of how you perceive money or those with money. As you can see with Harold, messages such as "money is evil" just serve to create a barrier between you and money. Someone who holds this belief will repel money and let go of it as quickly as it comes into his or her hands.

I keep coming back to ways to build your awareness, because only by understanding and questioning what you hold to be true can you break through blocks that keep you from real abundance. If this is an issue for you, try the following statement as your new thought pattern.

New Thinking for Self-Limiting Belief #3:
I Am Thankful for Money

GRATITUDE
I am thankful
for money.

PEACE OF MIND
I am at peace
with money.

THE ABUNDANCE LOOP

WISE CHOICES
I do my best and
allow money to flow.

POSITIVE OUTCOMES
I have a healthy
relationship with money.

I am thankful for money. See how this simple statement is a much more positive way to look at money in general? Here's one more example that I hope will help drive this point home. Perhaps you will see yourself or someone you know in Carol's story.

How Beliefs about Money Impact Your Life

Carol was often stressed about money. She would panic that she didn't earn enough and always seemed to be behind on her bills. She was tired of living that way and desperately sought to shift her relationship with her finances. I suggested that she write down all her beliefs about money. (After I tell you about her experience, you'll be able to try this exercise yourself.)

I gave Carol a piece of paper and had her write MONEY in large letters across the top. I asked her to write down all the words that came up for her as she thought about money. Her list looked like this: *scary, overwhelming, hate, questionable, scarce, hopeless, confusing,* and *risky.*

I then asked her about each word and how true it was. For example, she had written "scary" as one of her money beliefs. I asked her, "Is money itself scary?"

She replied, "No, but not having money is scary."

Look at the right-hand column in the following chart to see her responses when I inquired deeper into each of her beliefs:

Carol's Money Beliefs	How True Is This Money Belief? What Is Your Real Money Story?
Scary	Not having money is scary.
Overwhelming	Feeling like I don't have enough is overwhelming.
Hate	I hate not being able to have money.
Questionable	My financial future is questionable.
Scarce	Money is scarce. It's hard to come by. There's never enough.
Hopeless	I never make enough, so it seems hopeless.
Confusing	I don't know what to do with my money or my debt.
Risky	I need help managing the risks I take with my money.

Going through this exercise helped Carol realize that she didn't really feel those words about money itself, but about the lack of money. She immediately thought about the scarcity of money as opposed to the presence of money. Money itself didn't stress her, but not having enough did. Money itself wasn't confusing, but not knowing how to allocate her money was.

Separating the concept of "money" from her perspective of not having enough money really helped her clarify that money was not the main stressor in her life; it was her negative outlook, her scarcity mind-set, about money that was causing her to hate it and fight it. She had transferred the negative energy of her fear of not having enough money onto "money" itself.

In coaching Carol, I had her identify what was really negative and make space for a healthier relationship to money. I proceeded to help her gain clarity around her financial situation, which I will show you how to do later in this book. We laid out her assets, her liabilities, and her cash flow; and then we mapped out a plan to help her get out of debt.

After working with her to shift her awareness, challenge her beliefs, and lay out a concrete action plan, I then asked her to do the first exercise again and handed her another piece of paper. She wrote MONEY at the top, and this time, her words to describe money were *hopeful, excited, less stressed, ready to get the plan started, positive, clear, concrete, understanding,* and *focused.* She felt the powerful difference between her scarcity mind-set and one of abundance.

I followed up by asking her to write down and use these affirmations:

- *I have enough money.*

- *I have enough money to take care of my needs at this moment.*

- *I believe in my financial future.*

- *I am financially secure.*

- *I am abundant.*

- *I am building financial wealth.*

- *I am investing in myself.*

In less than an hour, Carol felt empowered enough to transform her relationship with money. She felt significantly better knowing that she had the power to change her beliefs around money and actually put together a plan. The act of writing out her financial situation, her savings (however minimal), debts (however looming and large), her income, and her expenses was cathartic. She felt happy to liberate her mind-set from the Scarcity Loop and excited about moving forward in the Abundance Loop.

EXERCISE:
Your Money Beliefs

Now it's your turn. Take your journal out and write the word MONEY in big letters across the top. Which words jump into your mind about money? Don't censor yourself. Allow yourself to jot down whatever words, phrases, or images that come to your mind, without judgment. There are no right or wrong words, just your truth. Give yourself time and space to let your thoughts flow. Some of what comes up might be scary or ugly—just let it flow.

Next, reflect on each word you wrote down. Ask yourself: *Is this how I truly feel about money itself? Or is it about the lack of money?*

I want you to notice how each word makes you feel. If the word makes you feel tense and constricted, write "ugghh" next to it. If the word makes you feel open and expansive, write "ahhhh" next to it.

Now tally up how many "ugghhs" you have compared to "ahhhhs." Don't be hard on yourself if your list of words is all negative. Facing your deep-seated beliefs with honesty and compassion requires a sincere effort. Take pride that you are doing it. You are unveiling the underlying mind-set that impacts your financial well-being.

The good news is that now you are starting to identify your fears so you can master them. By picking up this book and going through these exercises, you are taking a stand that you will no longer live in fear and confusion. You are in a position to take action to align with your best self. Celebrate this moment!

If most of your words give you a sense of relaxation and happiness, celebrate this wonderful blessing—you already have an abundance mind-set about money. You can move forward with gratitude, and you're ready to interact with money in a way that reflects your core values and to manifest wealth. And this book will show you how.

Developing an Abundance Mind-set

It's inspiring to hear this next story about Ava and how she was finally able to let go of her old beliefs and break free of her scarcity mind-set. The running script in her head about money was deeply held and very negative, like it is for so many of us, but Ava wanted a better life. She took the brave step to challenge and change her belief system about money and forge a path to financial security that she previously never thought was possible.

When I met her, Ava worked as a receptionist at the local university, where she was studying to earn a degree to become a marriage and family therapist. She was earning $25,000 a year, which was barely enough to cover her expenses. She was hopeful about her new career but couldn't imagine ever being financially rich.

When I asked her about how money was handled in her family, she recalled her parents sitting at the kitchen table going through the bills, completely worried and stressed-out about how they could only ever afford the minimum payments. Her mother used to always say, "I hate dealing with money."

Well, it's no wonder that when I asked Ava about her own financial aspirations, she responded, "I want to have enough to get by." I asked her how much "getting by" meant. She was looking forward to being a therapist and earning upward of about $80,000 a year. But she said that even if she made $50,000 a year, she'd be happy.

I asked her how she felt about earning $50K a year without even having to show up at work. She didn't understand. I clarified and asked would she want to potentially generate $50K a year in passive income so she could still work if she wanted to, but she wouldn't have to rely on working for money? She lit up. She didn't think that was even a possibility.

I explained to her that she would need to save about $800,000 to generate $50K a year in passive income. But, of course, she thought I was crazy. She said she would never be able to amass $800,000. Then I explained that since she had at least 40 more years in the workforce, all it would take was to save and invest $150 a month and slowly increase that as she made more money. Over time, she would be able to build an investment portfolio of that size.

Her eyes widened at that point, and I asked if she could do that right now. She said no—she could barely make ends meet. Then I asked her if she ever went shopping. Yes, she said, of course she did. "Do you ever buy anything you don't need?" I asked, and she acknowledged that yes, in fact, shopping was one of her guilty pleasures. Whenever she walked into a Target store, she felt the aisles calling to her. She loved to get lost in all the pretty clothes, bags, and accessories. She called it "retail therapy."

I asked her how much a typical retail-therapy session cost her at Target, and she admitted that she usually spent about $300 to $400 a month. I asked if she thought that she could cut that in half and put one half toward her retirement in a 401(k) at the university. She had never thought about that before.

The next day, she found out that her employer matched all employee contributions up to 6 percent. She decided to start contributing $150 a month to her 401(k) and build her savings, gradually increasing her investment over time. Ava made a bold step by starting to invest and grow her Money Tree, a concept that I describe in more detail for you in Step 6. Ava chose to create an abundant life, but in order to do so, she had to let go of her scarcity mind-set, the one that kept telling her she would only ever "get by."

To some degree, everyone is attached to scarcity. But like Ava, you can benefit by making a change in your belief systems, which will correspond with a change in behavior and a much more positive outcome. Rather than accept scarcity as just a part of who you are and how you live, declare, as Ava did, that you want to live differently and go for it.

EXERCISE:
Show Me the Money

Now it's your turn. This exercise is designed to help you raise your awareness about your relationship to money. As you work through the list of questions below, record your answers and at the same time, see if you can detect sensations in your body, maybe a twinge in your lower back, a tightness in your chest, or a constriction in your throat. Take a moment and ask yourself, *What is this sensation or emotion telling me?* Your body holds tremendous wisdom, and you can find answers to your questions by listening to it. Allow your body to speak to you as you think about these questions.

- How is money useful to you?

- How could more money be useful to you?

- What would you do if you had a million dollars?

- What would you do after that?

- How does having or not having money make you feel?

- How does spending money make you feel?

- What do you immediately want to do when you get money in your hands? Why?

- Is that really helpful to your life?

- What opportunities would more money give you?

- How could you help the world if you had more money?

- How would your relationships change if you had more money?

- How do your answers make you feel?

When your emotions or your body reacts to a strongly held belief in a negative way—such as with a wave of nausea, tightness, or constriction—that's a sign to you that it is no longer serving you. Think about how you can change those old beliefs and reframe them in a more positive way so that you are no longer constrained by old messages. Remember, the only limits you have are the ones you put on yourself.

Let Your Divine Shine

We will now face the greatest block of all: the ego. Letting go of your ego can get tricky because it has made you think it is *you*. Hence, this process is allowing your old self to die in order for your real self to come forward and live a glorious life. You only have a certain amount of resources and energy to expend in your life. You can use your energy, time, and money shoring up your image and strengthening your ego; or you can make a conscious choice to open your mind and accept that you are infinitely more than this scared, defensive persona you have created.

The ego represents the accumulation of thoughts and beliefs you hold about yourself, but as I described earlier, your ego is not truly who you are. Your ego is merely a false identity that you may have mistaken for yourself. It served you well growing up when you sought to survive in a confusing world, but as an adult, it gets in the way of embracing your divine wealth.

You may not recognize that the defended self you present to the world is a "story" because you're so deeply immersed in it—as the scriptwriter, director, and leading actor in your own life drama. But as long as you remain in the story that is being told by your ego, you will also remain stuck in the Scarcity Loop.

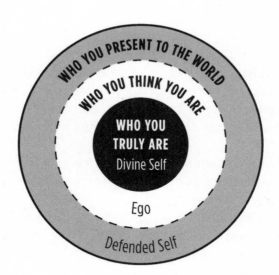

The diagram above illustrates the dynamic between the ego and the Divine Self. The outermost layer is the image we present to the world. We try to influence how others perceive us by looking, talking, and behaving in certain ways. We might invest precious time, money, and energy in our appearance, surroundings, and material possessions to soothe our egos and win acceptance from others . . . anything to make ourselves feel good about who we are.

However, the main focus of this book is not really on your ego or your defended self; it is on your Divine Self, shown in the center of the graphic. One very powerful way to bring out your true essence, which is your Divine Self, is to practice mindfulness or to meditate, as we talked about earlier. The closing exercise here is designed to help you connect even more closely with your Divine Self and divine abundance that is yours to discover and embrace.

EXERCISE:
Meditation to Align with Your Divine Abundance

This guided mediation takes the breathing exercises from earlier in this step to another level of increased awareness, this time focusing specifically on abundance. It might take some time and practice, but the more you do this kind of exercise, the easier it becomes for you to access your Divine Self and move out of scarcity and into true abundance in your daily life.

- *Sit in a comfortable position. Settle into your posture. Close your eyes. Relax your whole body. Bring awareness to your breath. Breathe in deeply and let it out slowly. As you gradually exhale, imagine your feet firmly planted into the ground. Like a tree with deep roots, you are connected to Mother Earth. Breathe out all the tension in your body into the earth's soil.*

- *As you inhale, allow the earth's energy to flow up slowly through your legs, your stomach, your chest, your throat, your head, and continuing up into the sky.*

- *Imagine the top of your head opening up and the sky filling every cell of your body with pure light. With each inhale, breathe in pure light. With each exhale, breathe out tension. Imagine you are grounded to the earth through your feet and connected to the heavens with pure light.*

- *As you continue to breathe and relax, imagine you are being transported to a place where everything feels calm and peaceful. What do you see? What sounds do you hear? What do you smell? How do you feel? Get a full sense of the feeling in your body.*

- *Now imagine Mother Earth, spirit, or someone you love cradling you and holding you securely with pure love and adoration. Know that you are completely safe in her embrace. Relax completely by focusing on your breathing. Exhale any tension that you may still be holding on to. You don't need it anymore.*

- *When you are fully relaxed and comforted in that perfect moment, imagine that every cell in your body is filled with peace and contentment that you have everything you need to be happy in this life. Listen to confirmation from Spirit that you are a divine being full of love, beauty, and abundance. You have all you need. It is a wonderful feeling.*

- *Know with certainty that you are enough. You feel this certainty with every fiber of your being and in every breath that you take. You adopt a new mantra for your life, and you repeat it with emotion and love: I am enough. I am enough. I am enough.*

- *Know with certainty that abundance is inside you and around you at all times. Feel it. Breathe it in. Feel the love and acceptance that you so richly deserve.*

- *Know with certainty that the sun rises each day to greet you with warmth and light so you can do your highest work. The world is waiting for you, the best you, to come forward and connect with it to create abundance for all. The world is complete because of your existence.*

- *Know with certainty that divine light shines on you, filling you with ideas and the power to manifest them. All the money and resources you need to fulfill your divine purpose flow to you daily. You feel whole and creative following your dreams and changing the world.*

- *Know with certainty that you are free to follow your heart's desires. The world supports you in fulfilling your dreams. As you move forward, everything you need falls into place. You feel so deeply grateful for these blessings.*

When you are ready, gradually return to your regular breathing, open your eyes if you had them closed, and come back to your surroundings, carrying with you the truth that you are a Divine Spirit who lives in abundance at all times.

This meditation is intended to help you create a secure and peaceful feeling and dispel many of the fears that keep you locked in scarcity. You are significantly more than who you think you are. This same feeling of being enough, of being amazing just for being you, can be yours at any time. Through practicing mindfulness and doing guided meditations like this, you will start to hold this feeling in your body and mind more and more deeply. You will come to accept that abundance *is* your natural birthright. It begins with you accepting that you are divinely loved just as you are right now. *You are enough.*

With this mind-set of abundance resonating inside you, and armed with techniques to update and replace your old beliefs, you are now ready to move on. In Step 3 of the Abundance Loop process, you will learn how to truly embrace gratitude for all that you are and all that you have.

Key Messages about Challenging Your Beliefs and Raising Your Awareness

- Quiet your mind by bringing attention to your breath. In stillness, you can access your divine wisdom.

- You *have* a body and you *have* thoughts—but "you" are the awareness of what happens in your body and your mind.

- Make room for abundance by reframing your self-limiting beliefs that keep you stuck in patterns of scarcity.

- You are infinitely more than who you think you are. Saying no to your ego is saying yes to your Divine Self.

- Align with your divine and experience peace and clarity.

STEP 3

Cultivate Gratitude

"How much money would you need to earn each year in order for you to feel rich?" I asked Oliver, a 21-year-old student who was working full-time to pay for his education.

"$80,000 to $100,000!" he immediately responded.

"Now imagine that you are earning $100,000 every year. Visualize receiving a paycheck for more than $8,000 month after month. How do you feel?"

A huge grin spread across his face. I could feel his palpable excitement as he said, "I feel amazing. I feel relieved. I'm happy and rich!"

I continued: "I'm so happy for you. You're finally earning your dream income that makes you feel rich. Congratulations. You've done it. Now, imagine that your best friend just texted you about his new job that will pay $1 million a year. Does that change how you feel?"

I could tell just by looking at him that it did. His face froze. He was now questioning himself and his dream salary of $100K.

Just a minute ago, he was feeling on top of the world and content. But on hearing how much his friend was making, now he wasn't so sure. Of course, Oliver started by saying he'd be happy for his friend, but then he admitted that he couldn't help but feel that maybe he (Oliver) didn't do something right. Maybe he aimed too low? Maybe $100K wasn't enough? But just two minutes ago, $100K brought him so much joy.

I shared with Oliver that it was normal to feel envy and second-guess himself. But the more he focused on his own benchmark and what was important to him, the less he would get triggered by what others had. By cultivating gratitude and feeling content with what he had, he could truly be happy for his friend and not let envy and fear of inadequacy taint the relationship.

Comparing ourselves to others has never been so easy, with social media sending us alerts and instant photos 24/7 of all the exciting things that our friends are doing. All of a sudden, we feel we want to buy something, go somewhere, or do something that others are doing, even when we hadn't cared to do it before.

Envy flares up when we least expect it and can be detrimental to both our net worth and our self-worth. Envy happens when you feel deep desire for what someone else has, and it robs you of your appreciation for what *you* have.

When you focus on what you lack, your self-worth begins to slide. To soothe your ego, you might then spend money or take unnecessary financial risks to try to match what you perceive that your peers have, even if your financial decisions have the potential to bring down your own net worth.

Envy is another aspect of life that keeps you in the Scarcity Loop. I have seen how keeping up with the Joneses causes both financial and emotional stress. But it doesn't have to. You can break free from this negative loop by cultivating gratitude, and that is what this step explains and explores.

Gratitude Gets You In

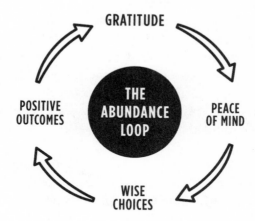

As you have seen already and are reminded of above, the Abundance Loop begins with gratitude. When you shift your awareness and attention to what is available to you, you begin to see how much you have to be grateful for. When you feel deep gratitude, you experience peace of mind. When you let go of the "but I don't have" feelings, and all the things you can't do or that you feel you "just need to have," then you can viscerally sense that you actually do have everything you need right in this very moment. With a calmer and more peaceful mind, you make better decisions that will most likely lead to the results you want. Once you manifest your desires, you return to the top of the loop—a place of gratitude—and the circle continues.

Giving Thanks Is Good for You

We've all been trained by our parents, schools, and religious organizations to say "Thank you." The value of giving thanks has been recognized and taught by cultures around the world for millennia. It is the moral and polite thing to do. The process of feeling and expressing gratitude is now studied scientifically, and the data shows that an attitude of gratitude also correlates positively with our level of happiness.

I interviewed Dacher Keltner, professor of psychology at the University of California, Berkeley, and founding director of the Greater Good Science Center, who shared the following: "The world conspires to make us chase the illusion that happiness is found in material advance and consumerism, when in fact the science shows that it is our connections, our generosity, and our sense of being fulfilled by what we have that is the best pursuit of happiness."

Scientists are continually researching the benefits of gratitude. Recent studies have shown that people who practice it experience better overall health. Grateful people experience higher levels of positive emotions—more joy, optimism, alertness, and pleasure. They are also less lonely, more compassionate, and more outgoing.

Gratitude helps to block toxic and negative emotions such as envy, resentment, and regret—emotions that can destroy happiness. According to a study by Dr. Robert Emmons, a leading scientific expert on gratitude at the University of California, Davis, grateful thinking can increase happiness by as much as 25 percent. He found that keeping a gratitude journal, even for as little as three weeks, results in better sleep and more energy. Participants who kept gratitude lists were more likely to have made progress toward important personal goals than those who didn't keep lists.[1] Personally, I am a fan of gratitude, so you will find several practical exercises in this step to help you master an attitude of gratitude.

Not surprisingly, when we are happy, we tend to be more productive, creative, sociable, and energized, which opens us up to opportunities for higher income, longer and more satisfying relationships, deeper friendships, greater self-control and coping abilities, a bolstered immune system, less pain, less stress, and increased longevity.[2] The benefits of gratitude and happiness are definitely wide-ranging and, in my mind, worth cultivating.

EXERCISE:
Expressing Gratitude

Because gratitude is the basis of the Abundance Loop and I truly want you to embrace it, I am presenting various kinds of exercises so you can practice expressing it using whichever learning style you prefer.

- **For Visual Learners:** Stop for a moment and slowly take a look around you. Observe everything you see and notice all that is available to you. If you're at home, you can appreciate the chair or bed you're resting on, the clothes you're wearing, and the roof over your head. Even if you're in the bathroom, you can take a moment to appreciate indoor plumbing, toilet paper, running water, a working shower, shampoo, and soft towels. If you're outside, you can appreciate the sun, the sky, and the trees. Wherever you are—in your car, at work, in a line at the store— simply acknowledge how blessed you are in this very moment.

- **For Aural Learners:** If you learn best through listening, then take in all the different sounds available to you in this very moment. Listen to the wide range of pitches, voices, and background murmurs. Be thankful for the music you may hear playing in the background. When outside, stop and listen to the sounds of nature, of laughing children, of dogs barking and birds singing. Soak in the richness of life through your ears and feel truly blessed and thankful for all the magic this world offers.

- **For Read-Write Learners:** This is a simple but powerful way to become more thankful: Complete a nightly journal exercise by writing down three blessings you enjoyed that day—things that you were grateful for—and do this consistently at least for three weeks in a row. It takes 21 days to form a habit, so once the first three weeks are up, keep on going. Another simple exercise is to write a thank-you note to someone. Let the recipient know what it is that you truly appreciate about him or her and how blessed you feel that this person is in your life.

- **For Verbal Learners:** Tell someone how much you appreciate him or her. Whenever someone holds the door for you, say "thank you" and take a moment to truly feel appreciation for that person. Before a meal, give a few words of thanks for the food you are about to eat that will nourish your body. Get in the habit of expressing gratitude to people; pets; plants; and even inanimate objects such as your bed, your car, and the money you do have.

- **For Kinesthetic Learners:** Reach for something near you and hold it in your hands. Whether it's a warm cup of coffee, your wallet, an iPhone, or a flower, take a moment and feel how blessed you are to touch this object. Hug someone—maybe your pet, your child, or your friend. I was on the plane and desperately wanted to finish this book. But my two-year-old son fell asleep on me during takeoff. The irony was not lost on me that I wanted to spend the one-hour flight writing about gratitude, but instead, I had this amazing opportunity to appreciate his warm embrace. As he lay his sweet head on my chest, I just stared at his sleeping face and tears streamed down my face. I thanked God for this beautiful child in my arms. I thought of how quickly he is growing, and I soaked in the precious moment of his little body resting so peacefully on me for the entire flight.

Also for Kinesthetic Learners: Take a deep breath and move. Move your head, shoulders, arms, and feet. Allow yourself to feel your body. Get up and dance if you can, sway your hips, and feel the power you hold in your body. Give thanks for the body that you are in now, without thinking about what you wish you could change. Quiet your inner critic as you lovingly focus on the body you have now, for it is changing every day.

Touch your skin, your hair, your fingers, and your eyes. Be thankful for the complex yet elegant system that keeps you breathing, moving, and processing the world with your senses, and for the billions of cells working perfectly without you being conscious of it. Take a moment and feel gratitude for your knees that hold you up, for your feet that carry you everywhere, for your arms, your hands, and your neck.

Give thanks to every part of you that makes up the beautiful and divine being that you are in this very moment. We always have something to do, somewhere to be, someone else to meet. Time moves so quickly, but if you can be present and appreciate each moment, you experience the abundance of true wealth.

The Happiness Formula

Many of us constantly modify our external circumstances in the hope of becoming happy. Psychologist Martin Seligman devised a formula to illustrate that we have the situation backward. Known as the father of positive psychology, Seligman believes that our enduring level of happiness is the sum of our genetic set point for happiness, our life circumstances, and our voluntary control of our thoughts and actions. Yes, there are those thoughts and actions again. Let's see how this theory works in relation to what we already know about thoughts and actions:

Happiness = Genetic Set Point (50%) + Circumstances (10%) + Voluntary Control (40%)

Seligman states that our genetic capacity for happiness is relatively fixed. We inherited the natural temperament that we did, and we can't do much to change the genetic set point part of the equation, which makes up 50 percent. So let's delve into the other 50 percent that we do have control over: circumstances (10 percent of the happiness equation) and our thoughts and actions (40 percent).[3]

Most of us spend significant time, money, and energy on changing our life circumstances to increase our happiness. We anxiously try to update our living conditions, the clothes we wear, the cars we drive, and the partners we share our lives with. Nonetheless, our circumstances only make up 10 percent of the happiness formula, so we really can't effect much change in our level of satisfaction in these ways.

Getting a raise or a new job, entering a new relationship, or winning the lottery does spike your level of happiness, but not for long, it turns out. Studies show that even lottery winners come back to the initial level of happiness they had prior to their windfall just about two years after winning a big jackpot. On the other hand, those who have an optimistic mind-set quickly regain their happiness baseline even after serious setbacks. This is because they leverage what we do have more control over (40 percent)—our mind-set and actions.

You have control over your thoughts. Although you can't always control what pops up in your mind, you have the choice whether to hold on to that thought or let it go. You can choose what to think about. When your mind wanders, you have the ability to bring it back to the present.

You also have power over your actions. When someone triggers you in a certain way, you can choose how to react. You can't change another person or control his or her actions; however, you do have full control over whether to engage in the conversation or walk away.

You no doubt know someone whom you would love to change. Maybe the person acts in ways that annoy you or hurt you, but unless that person has the desire and willingness to change, you are wasting your time and energy trying to get him or her to behave differently.

With the power of choice, you take on the responsibility for your own actions. I can't emphasize enough the importance of being conscious of the choices you are making with your thoughts and actions. We will dive more deeply into choices and actions later in the book. Meanwhile, let's look at how changing your internal state can transform your life.

Turn Your Life Inside Out

It's easy to wait for something on the outside to change before you become happy. You can try to manipulate external factors to fix your internal emotions, but it doesn't really work. You can wait to make more money, or for your partner to do something nice, or for whatever circumstances you may be facing to settle down before you relax and enjoy life. In the meantime, your happiness is on edge, waiting for something to change, and your emotions fluctuate with daily occurrences.

But let's flip this around and consider what would happen if you operated from the inside out instead of the outside in. What I mean is what if you stabilize your internal state so you can navigate through daily activities and design the life you want?

It's easier than you think to accomplish this, and gratitude is the key. Instead of waiting for something externally in your life to change, you can simply acknowledge what is and be grateful. This doesn't mean you just lie down like a doormat and accept whatever happens to you. Not at all.

Instead, I'm suggesting that you develop a stronger ability to stand in your divine truth and learn to better handle what comes your way. With practice you will become more confident in this quest. Eventually you will find that outside events and people don't rock you the way they used to because now you are aware that your fears are being triggered, and it's just your ego that wants to spring into action.

Once you understand that you are not your ego, you can exercise your inner resources and break free from it and embrace your authentic self. With gratitude for the person you are, you can learn to keep your old fears from being triggered. You can act differently by choice. How hugely liberating!

Here's an example of a difficult day from my own life where I had to practice using gratitude and not reacting to old fears. It started when my husband snapped at me while our two-year-old son was screaming at the top of his lungs in the middle of a parking lot. I knew mentally that my husband was just frustrated that the baby was throwing a tantrum and that I was not really to blame.

Nonetheless, the fact that he took it out on me still hurt. My ego kicked in and I immediately fell into my old defensive patterns of shutting down, ignoring my husband, and going grizzly-mama on my baby while keeping him away from his father. Meanwhile, I felt a battle going on inside me. My ego so desperately wanted to shut me down, wallow in victimhood, quietly hate my husband, and hurt him by fleeing with our son. It was an old pattern I was very used to following, and I struggled with breaking free of it.

Meanwhile, my Divine Self observed the situation from a witness standpoint and came up with a new way of handling things. I heard my own wisdom telling me: *You know these tactics are making it worse. You know he loves you, and he didn't mean to yell at you. Just communicate your feelings to him calmly instead of spiraling downward.* I remember being shocked at this internal advice, but it rang true, and I could see it was a healthier interaction.

Once we were away from the public, I was still seething a bit, but then my husband broke the thick silence and thanked me for taking care of our son. I give him huge credit for making the first move with an overture of gratitude. Instead of simply saying

"You're welcome" and forgetting about my pain, I calmly admitted that his yelling scared me and triggered old wounds and made me feel really awful inside. He then shared how he was hurt that I ignored him and pulled the baby away from him. We both apologized. I realized how this approach helped to heal the wound instead of letting it fester, which is what I used to do in the past.

By developing greater self-awareness, I was able to recognize my ego at work, and I consciously chose not to fall into old, destructive patterns. By opening myself and being more honest with my feelings and expressing how I felt, I was able to turn that interaction around so it became a chance for us to deepen our love and gratitude for each other. And although it didn't feel like we were in the Abundance Loop at the time, I realized afterward how we created more trust and abundance in our relationship by risking our emotions and aligning with our best selves.

Fear and Gratitude in the Stock Market

So you can see how gratitude arises when you acknowledge what you already have, as opposed to craving something you lack. When you take stock of every blessing you have earned or have been given, your present moment is filled with the energy of abundance. You place your attention on the positive, which expands your heart and mind so you can soak up all that life offers. As you experience this enlivening energy of bountifulness, you'll find that your attachment to material goods, jealousy, resentment, and anxiety diminishes. Contrast this with what happens when you concentrate on the negative aspects of your life, such as things you don't have or don't like. Focusing only on the negative causes your physical and spiritual energy to contract.

I see this contraction and expansion principle at work in my wealth-advisory practice every day. Clients tend to let their sense of abundance fluctuate with the stock market. Financial security does rely on positive returns, yes, but not at the risk of significant loss of money or peace of mind. You can achieve your financial goals with slow and steady growth while being able to sleep at night. This requires the resolve to be grateful for what you have, a well-balanced portfolio that is designed to meet your needs, as opposed to constantly chasing a high-flying stock or a market index such as the S&P 500 or the Dow Jones.

I can see that it's tempting to chase the highest returns, especially when you're driven by fear or greed and caught up in the belief that you don't have enough. But when you operate in the Abundance Loop, you can maintain your equanimity regardless of how the markets are doing. You don't need to react impulsively when you have an inner knowing that you *have* enough and that you *are* enough. The calmness you feel helps you make the best investment decisions for you, without fear or anxiety, and your portfolio can grow without the drama or sleepless nights. Let's expand on this idea of returning to calmness and peace by learning some more practical ways to be grateful.

EXERCISE:
Practical Techniques to Increase Your Gratitude

There are so many wonderful ways you can boost your gratitude, and they are easy to weave into your daily life. Here are just a few of my favorite techniques that work for my clients and me.

- **Give Thanks as Soon as You Wake Up.** Simple thoughts about waking up in a warm bed or having running water will help you start your day in a positive frame of mind.

- **Give Thanks Before You Fall Asleep.** Acknowledging the simple fact that you have a roof over your head and a safe place to sleep can put your mind at ease.

- **Sign Every E-mail "With Gratitude."** These two simple words not only inspire you to be grateful, but also let the recipients know how much you value them. This allows for a more positive rapport.

- **Tell People How Much You Appreciate Them.** When you thank others, you've given them the opportunity to feel good about themselves. You are helping to increase both your self-worth (you received value from them) and theirs (they had value to share).

- **Quiet Your Mind, Meditate, and Pray.** The techniques from the previous step are hugely powerful because you learn to place your attention on all that you have and all that you are. Imagine being connected to the abundant resources of the universe and give thanks for that connection.

- **Share with Others.** Whether you're offering food, money, time, or a simple act of kindness, share yourself and your abundance with others. Sharing what you have naturally proves that you had more than enough to begin with. Acts of generosity reinforce your Abundance Loop, while sowing seeds of gratitude so others can experience their own Abundance Loop.

EXERCISE:
Your Abundant Life

Let's get more specific about what it is you have to be thankful for. Begin by finding a space to write or record your ideas. Take a few moments to relax, shake off any tension, and breathe deeply.

At the top of the page, write down today's date and the title: "My Abundant Life."

Start by going through your typical day, beginning with the moment you wake up in the morning. Below are some prompts to help you get going, but feel free to write about anything you feel blessed by, focusing on the positive things in your life. Include what you might think are small or simple things like your pillow or your warm pajamas, while also making note of the bigger things in your life like your home and your family.

For this exercise, don't include anything that you actually don't have yet. I know that there are always more and nicer things to acquire, but the point of this exercise is to focus on how much you have already. Also, try your best to focus on the positive and keep the "buts" out. For instance, you can say, "I have a car," and stop before you say, "but I wish it was nicer."

If you get stuck, try starting off your sentences with "I am thankful that . . ." Take your time. There's no need to rush through this. Ready? Set? Go.

My Abundant Life

- I wake up to _____.

- In my bathroom, I have _____.

- In my closet, I have _____.
- In my kitchen, I have _____.
- I love my [*or* that I can]_____.
- I have a mode of transportation _____.
- On my commute, I get to_____.
- I have a job that _____.
  (*Remember to stay positive!*)
- I have the time to_____.
- I have the ability to _____.
- I have enough money to _____.
  (*Think what you <u>can</u> do, not <u>cannot</u>!*)
- I have a phone to connect with_____.
- I have family that _____.
  (*Note just the positive things!*)
- I have friends who _____.
- I have my health so I can _____.
- I find joy in _____.
- For dinner, I eat _____.
- In my community, I have _____.
- Where I live, I have _____.
- At the end of the day, I _____.
- I am _____and abundant!

Congratulations for documenting your abundant life! Simply by recording it, you are acknowledging how much you have right now. Well done! Now that you've taken inventory of all the things you are thankful for, how do you feel? Do you notice a difference in your mental state by having gone through this exercise? What shifted for you? How can you channel this newfound energy into your life?

I like to revisit this list, and I encourage you to do the same on a regular basis and continue to add to your abundant life.

The Marshmallow Test

Back in the 1960s, Stanford psychologist Walter Mischel conducted a study on self-control with a group of children about five years old. The researcher presented each child with a plateful of treats and the choice to have one marshmallow now or two marshmallows later if he or she could wait almost 20 minutes. As expected, some children ate the marshmallow immediately while others used all sorts of tactics to distract themselves from eating the treat right away.

I ran this experiment a few years ago when my older son was four. I tried my best to contain my laughter as I listened to him moan, watched him pull his hair out, and stare longingly at the marshmallow before petting it and then finally licking it. I was disheartened that he didn't have more willpower because I already knew the long-term results of the study.

Researchers followed some of these children over their lifetimes and found that those who had waited to double their payoff scored higher on their SATs, lived healthier lifestyles, earned more money in adulthood, and had a greater sense of self-worth than those who indulged in the single marshmallow right away.

What can we learn from this? Self-control is an essential requirement to achieving success. Whether your goal pertains to your career, your health, your relationships, or your finances, you must flex your willpower muscle and learn to delay gratification. And practicing gratitude is a healthy way to stave off your impulses.

Imagine how different your life would be if you could consistently behave in ways that produce the outcomes you want. What if you could walk through Target, Macy's, or Nordstrom without taking out your credit card? Instead of moving through life saying, "I gotta have that," imagine the feeling if your mental dialogue repeatedly sang, *I have all that I need.*

In the next few pages, I will share tips on how to control your spending without feeling deprived, ashamed, or guilty. I'm not here to handcuff you and restrain you from doing what you want. On the contrary, my goal is to help you transform yourself from being a trapped consumer to a wise investor.

From Consumer to Investor

Your mind-set is the primary driver of your actions. Let's look at the thoughts of a consumer versus those of an investor and see if you recognize yourself in any of them. Awareness of your thoughts must come before you can change them. If you find that you are more of a consumer than an investor, consider adopting a new mind-set. Try asking yourself the questions that investors would ask of themselves.

CONSUMER	INVESTOR
I can't wait. I need to buy this now.	I can wait. I don't need to buy this right now.
I don't have the time or patience to research this. Let me just buy now.	I have time to carefully research this so I don't make any rash decisions.
I need this.	Do I really need this?
How much can I spend?	How much can I save?
I don't care how much this costs. Let me get it now while I'm here. Time is money.	I love this, but I'll wait for it to go on sale. Meanwhile, I can let my money grow.
It's okay that I waste money. I can always make more.	How can I make this last? I don't want to waste money.
How fast can I spend this?	How long can I make this last?
I want to buy what my friends have.	That's great my friends have that, but I don't need it.
I can't withstand the ups and downs of the market. I could have gone on vacation with the money I lost in stock values last year. I'm pulling out.	I can afford to ride out the bumps in the market. I have a long-term perspective and don't intend to touch the money for a while.
How can I spend my money?	How can I save and invest my money?
I need to earn more to spend more.	I need to earn more to invest more.
How much can I spend for myself?	How much can I leave for the next generation?
How much can I keep for myself?	How much can I share with others?

In summary, consumers think about spending what they don't have. Investors think about growing what they already have. Although the questions in the table relate mostly to money, please note that you can choose to be a consumer or an investor of your life and of this planet. Being invested in your life means you're aligned with your divine—you're stepping forward and showing up to be the best you can be. You help this world by sharing the unique gifts that only you have.

The Abundance of Now

Regardless of where you are in the process of learning about abundance, it's worth thinking about happiness with regard to this very moment. The following story illustrates that abundance exists now but overcoming the resistance to it isn't always easy, especially when we are so focused on the past and the future.

I recently met with a 35-year-old named Mark who was frustrated that he wasn't earning as much money as he would like. He described himself as "standing on the precipice of happiness." He felt that he was close to being happy but not there yet. He was so used to being stressed-out and worried about things falling apart that he was afraid to relax. Despite his attachment to his anxiety about the future, I engaged him in a conversation about the present moment. Here's what our dialogue looked like:

JP: How do you feel about getting up and going to work?

Mark: I love the people I work with. I just wish I was getting paid more.

JP: How do you feel about where you live?

Mark: The apartment itself needs some sprucing up and nicer furniture, but the neighborhood is great, with fun places to hang out.

JP: How do you feel about the new woman you're seeing?

Mark: So far, she seems to be everything I'm looking for, but I don't want to get my hopes up.

JP: What are you worried about?

Mark: That it'll all go south. Something will blow up—it always does.

As I sat across from him, I saw how his fear and frustration made him uneasy, and the tension was getting in the way of his enjoying the present moment. His nervous energy was apparent in his hand movements, tense facial expression, and inability to sit still. We don't see it, but we all emit energy. Our emotions and thoughts live in our bodies, and this energy seeps out of our bodies into a field around us.

I wanted to help Mark shift his mind-set from one of scarcity to one of abundance. I asked him to focus on what he had that he was grateful for. He shared with me that he recently went to his parents' home, where he cleared out a box of his old stuff. He saw a paper that he had written in high school about what he wanted to be when he grew up. He was shocked to recall that he wanted to be in the banking industry and that he was actually in the job that he envisioned 20 years ago!

We then turned to his personal life. He could hardly believe that he was dating this stunning woman and was shocked that she was truly interested in him. As he put aside the complaints and solely looked at what he actually had, Mark realized that he in fact did have a pretty good life. By golly, he was even, dare he say it, "almost happy."

Almost?! I felt like I was pulling teeth to get him to appreciate his life in its current form, so I had him look at his life again. He was working in the job he dreamed of as a kid, he had his own apartment in a hip part of town, and he was seeing a woman he could envision having a family with. He writhed uncomfortably in his seat and resisted for a few minutes, but he finally admitted to me, "Okay, you did it. You got it out of me. I'm happy, god-damn it. I'm just not used to saying that I'm happy." He could barely look at me. As a matter of fact, as soon as he said it, he ran to the restroom.

When Mark returned, I suggested to him that when he wakes up in the morning, he should start the day by getting off the precipice of happiness and announce to himself that he's already arrived by declaring, "I am happy now."

I've followed up with him after that meeting, and he still wakes up happy. He admitted that some days it takes more effort than others, but he reminds himself that he has the ability to shift his perspective. Like Mark, you don't need to wait to be happy. You can be happy now.

Life is a series of *nows*, not *laters*. Waiting to be happy is essentially proclaiming that you are unhappy now. And the experience you feel in this present moment is what matters. Create a lifetime of happiness by relishing the abundance of now.

Creating the Space to Appreciate Abundance

One very practical way that you can be happier is to keep your home and office tidy. You have control over your environment. Your decision to leave papers strewn all over your floor or throw them away directly impacts your physical space, which influences your mind.

Dealing with money can be stressful enough as is, so I recommend that you create a peaceful dedicated space just for you to work and deal with your finances. Remember, you want to get to "ahhhh." Well, it's hard to feel "ahhhh" when your room is overrun with old magazines, piles of bills, endless filing from long ago, and an ever-growing collection of stuff.

It's time to check your excuses and your ego at the door. Tell yourself that you are in charge, and take control of the chaos. Get rid of what you don't need and create the environment that you want. You have the power to design your space to evoke a sense of "ahhhh" each and every time you sit down to do your finances or your work.

Researchers at Princeton University Neuroscience Institute found that clutter in your environment distracts your brain from processing information and limits your ability to focus.

Whether the story is, "I don't have enough time to deal with this bill now," or "I may need this information later," piles of paper can signal that you are getting stuck again in that dreaded Scarcity Loop.

EXERCISE:
Gratefully Clearing the Clutter

If your home office or the corner desk where you pay your bills is a disaster, your finances may well follow suit. When you can calm the chaos of your physical space, you feel more inclined to bring that peace into your financial affairs as well. Here are some practical tips to help bring out the tidy person lurking inside you:

- Consciously go through your desk and boxes with an attitude of gratitude as you clean them up.

- When throwing away receipts or filing them, say: "I truly enjoyed that meal with my friend" (or the item you purchased).

- When putting away coffee mugs, pens, and other things, say: "I am happy to have an organized home."

- Take two minutes each week to clear out the receipts from your purse or wallet.

- When you have paper money, don't crumple it up. Make it a habit to treat money well and line up the bills neatly in your wallet.

- Take five minutes at the end of each day to straighten up or sort through one pile of your paperwork, and then congratulate yourself for doing so.

- Toss any scraps of paper or envelopes you don't need, and throw away any pens that don't work well, reminding yourself that these items have served their purpose.

- If you have items in your office or house you no longer need, donate them to charity. Tell yourself as you pack up the box of items to give away: *I enjoyed having this item, and I am glad to share it with another person.*

- Notice the difference you feel in the energy of a place that is clean and organized. Be grateful for your tidy space.

Key Messages about Cultivating Gratitude

- Envy robs you of your appreciation for what *you* have.

- Be grateful for all that you have, all that you are, and all that you have yet to experience.

- Only 10 percent of your happiness comes from your external circumstances. You control 40 percent of your happiness with your thoughts and actions.

- Consumers spend what they don't have. Investors grow what they already have.

- Life is a series of present moments. Live in the abundance of now.

- Make space in your environment to let abundance flow.

STEP 4

Clarify Your Values and Intentions

I meditated frequently in the midst of my divorce in 2010. It certainly helped me feel less stressed, and I was much better able to cope with all the changes in my life at the time. I gained tremendous insights, too, and I would like to share one particularly vivid experience.

One day, while I was in a beautiful meditative state, I saw that I was scuba diving, something that I have never actually done in real life. I was exploring uncharted waters and taking in the brilliant colors of the tropical fish swimming around me. I thought, *This is what everyone calls paradise.*

At first, the novelty of being underwater excited me, but it started to dissipate as I felt the weight of my body moving sluggishly. As I navigated through the murkier parts, I thought that although many people might love this experience, I did not. I got out of the water and stepped onto a beach.

As I removed the diving mask, heavy tank, and breathing apparatus, I felt lighter. I welcomed the fact that my vision cleared up, and I enjoyed breathing the fresh air. I imagined hearing the fun sounds of a steel-drum band playing in the distance. I kicked off the imaginary fins and loved feeling the support of the warm sand beneath my feet. I drank in the magnificent hues and fresh scents of the flowers and was ecstatic to imagine a table full of fresh fruit. I reached for an orange with both hands and tasted the juiciest fruit.

When I reflected back on this meditation experience, I realized that for me, paradise is being on a beach eating fresh foods. Everyone has his or her *own* opinions and desires. Although many people might love scuba diving, I didn't. My meditation reinforced my belief that I must develop the courage and clarity to discover what I truly want and go for it.

I was now aware of how liberating and wonderfully juicy my life could be when it reflects my values and preferences without the heavy armor that I had been clinging to for survival. I didn't need to hide behind a mask, nor did I need to breathe through an awkward contraption. I could take away all that "stuff" and feel free to trust myself and follow my heart.

I share this story to illustrate that it's important to make your own judgments about what matters to you and what you want. If you are not living in alignment with your core values, and you are not living as you want to be, then you are, at least to some degree, in danger of wasting your precious assets of time, money, and energy. You are in danger of wasting your most valuable gift— *your life*.

Step 4 consists of stories and exercises designed to help you discover your own core values and intentions, so you can allocate your precious resources to the parts of your life that are most important to you.

What Matters Most

Regardless of your age and stage in life, clarifying your core values is always beneficial because they serve as your true north. This was certainly the case for a young woman who was part of my life a few years ago.

One foggy morning (which is every summer morning in the Bay Area), I sat down with Lacy, who wanted help in figuring out her career path. After listening to her describe her many different interests, I gave Lacy a Post-it pad and asked her to write down what she deeply cared about on each individual sheet. I wanted her to think about everything she values.

She applied herself to the task, writing down one value at a time, and plastered the wooden surface of the table with 30 small yellow sheets. We reviewed each word and acknowledged that every one of these core values was important to her. However, for the purposes of this exercise, I asked her to put the five "least essential" of her values aside. Then another five aside. And another five. She kept going until she couldn't whittle away any more.

Lacy discovered that her core values at that time included family, connection with community, reading, teaching, and gymnastics. She mentioned that a few years ago, she could have easily narrowed it down to just gymnastics. She explained that the gym had been her second home, and her team became her second family since she was seven years old. She practiced 25 hours a week during the school year and 40 hours a week during summers and vacations. She earned many medals, including state and regional championships, and was preparing to join a college team when she severely injured her back and was forced to quit.

During her long recovery, Lacy could barely walk, gained 20 pounds, and fell into a depression. She grappled with her self-worth and identity, and she started to loathe herself. Who *was* she off the gymnastics team? Did she have any value if she could no longer compete? Without her coaches and teammates, who would understand her and support her to be her best? She spent many weeks crying in bed wondering if there was any purpose to her life.

Then something amazing happened. Friends from school, the neighborhood, and her church came to visit her, sitting by her side and hanging out with her. She learned the video game that her brother played, and they developed a stronger relationship. She improved her chess game enough to beat her dad. She read a ton of books and started volunteering as an English tutor and discovered a new passion for teaching. Most importantly, she started to feel her self-worth rise again.

The painful experience of hitting rock bottom pushed her to assess who she was outside of the gym and outside of her own ego. It took some time, but Lacy shifted out of her Scarcity Loop and discovered how abundant life could be after the competitions and medals stopped. She realized that what matters most to her now, outside her family, is living a purposeful life, teaching, and building a deep connection with her community. The values exercise motivated her to apply to organizations such as Teach For America.

Who Are You Really?

Like Lacy, you might feel unsure of who you are and what you want when your foundation has been shaken. Your extreme attachment to your identity as an athlete, student, doctor, musician, or even parent can get in the way of knowing who and what you truly are and what you can become.

All too often, we lose sight of our essential selves. We think we "are" our interests and confuse our appearance, role, fame, wealth, material possessions, accolades, or career with who we are. But when this changes, which it invariably does, we may end up believing that we're worthless without those accomplishments, abilities, and other external trappings.

Fortunately, you don't have to wait for a medical crisis, or to hit rock bottom financially or in your relationships, to identify what you care about most. When you take the time to figure out what resonates deeply with you, you can follow your own beacon of light to guide your choices and actions to create an abundant life in a personally meaningful way.

Transfer Values Before Wealth

What would it be like to suddenly be wildly rich? Although many people dream of hitting the lottery or winning big at the casino, life doesn't seem to end "happily ever after" for most lottery winners or beneficiaries of inherited wealth. Big winners seem to fall victim to irrational behaviors after the sudden infusion of funds. Their deep-seated beliefs that they are not worthy of abundance, or their shame and guilt, often interfere with their ability to make sound financial choices.

Likewise, those who inherit wealth have their own challenges. Seventy percent of the time, wealth never makes it to the third generation.[1] In Italy, they have an expression: "First generation creates the wealth, second generation inherits, third generation destroys." In China, people say, "Rice paddies to rice paddies in three generations." The first generation starts off poor, building wealth from the rice paddies. The second generation inherits the wealth and moves away from the rice paddies into the big city, and spends all or most of their inheritance. With little money left, the third generation returns to the rice paddies. In the U.S., we have a similar saying, "Shirtsleeves to shirtsleeves in three generations." Money in families just doesn't seem to sustain itself more than two generations. Studies show that the primary reason behind this global phenomenon isn't excessive taxation or poor investment management, but poor family communication.

Most people aren't used to taking the time to clarify what they truly value. Hence, parents typically don't communicate their values to their children, especially around money. After transferring their genes, parents focus on transferring their wealth by purchasing toys, clothes, and cars for their children, and financing college education, apartments, and even their ongoing lifestyles. Yet without the transferring of values, the money—however much is passed to the next generation—will likely disappear.

Wealth psychologists Joan DiFuria and Dr. Stephen Goldbart formed the Money, Meaning & Choices Institute (MMCI) to specifically facilitate communication within wealthy families, especially between siblings and across generations. MMCI developed a process that begins with a six-hour-long values retreat, where they gather the different family members and mediate a discussion about their money issues, priorities, and passions. By asking a series of questions, such as, "Why is that important to you? And for what purpose?" each person is able to arrive at his or her own core values. After MMCI white-boards all the different words and phrases, the family then edits the wording and agrees on shared values to create the family's Core Values Statements. Family members can always refer back to this living document to help guide their financial decisions.

When I interviewed DiFuria, she emphasized that value statements of any kind had to be in a person's own language and "livable," meaning that the person must be able to act the values out in her or his life. Values held in common across successful families included family unity, spirituality and religion, self-care, financial literacy, and a shared interest in having fun.

DiFuria recommended that once values statements were written exactly the way a family wanted, they should be posted somewhere everyone could routinely see them, such as on a refrigerator or in the living room. They should be visible so that all members of the family could be reminded regularly about what was truly important to everyone.

DiFuria and Goldbart also wrote a book (which I highly recommend) called *Affluence Intelligence* to share their findings regarding the best practices of how to earn more, worry less, and live a happy life. (For additional information to support your financial and personal growth, please see the Resources section and Appendix in the back of this book or visit my website: www.julianapark.com.)

EXERCISE:
Figuring Out Your Own Core Values

You knew it was coming. Yes, now it's your turn to discover your own core values. I've done this five-step exercise many times with different people and am always delighted to see individuals discover what matters most to them. The best way is to do this is to use Post-it notes or set of index cards, because they are easy to move around—but writing the words down in your journal, on your laptop, or even on the back of a napkin can work as well. Plan to spend about 20 minutes.

Once you complete this exercise, be aware that you can use your Core Values Statement to come up with financial values as well, and then use those financial values to make sound choices with regard to earning, spending, saving, and sharing your money.

1. Quiet Your Mind. To begin, you will want to tap into your Divine Self and the best way to do that is by quieting your mind following the breathing exercises you practiced in Step 2. Take a few moments to shake off any tension and plant your feet onto the ground. Feel the earth supporting you as you straighten your back, sit tall, and take a deep breath. Bring your attention to your breathing and simply allow the inner chatter to quiet down. Remember, you have the power to dismiss thoughts that pop into your head. Focus on saying, "I am letting it go. I am letting it all go." Repeat as many times as needed to relax and come into the present moment. When you feel ready, then proceed.

2. Write Down Your Core Values. Take your Post-it pad or index cards and start jotting down a simple phrase or word on each sheet of paper. Don't worry about getting every word exactly right. Your goal here is to identify what matters to you. You want to let your ideas flow, so don't censor yourself. If your inner critic wants to insert itself in the process, telling you, "You should list . . ." or "You can't write that!" say that you're not available now and you'll get back to him or her later. Be gentle with yourself. Just keep moving forward. Write down as many core values as you can, even if they don't seem to be a top priority at this point. Here are some questions to consider, as they might help you rev up the engine of your mind:

- *What are your lifestyle values?* Some examples might include traveling the world to experience different cultures, being productive in a job, getting a certain kind of education, creating art, taking care of yourself (physically, emotionally, and mentally), taking care of the environment, and spending quality time with family.

- *What characteristics do you admire in others?* Examples include sense of humor, courage, loyalty, dependability, honesty, cleanliness, flexibility, respect, integrity, teamwork, and so on.

- *Which activities or "ways of being" do you value?* Examples include serving people in less fortunate communities, cooking healthy meals, caring for others, meditating, playing soccer, and engaging in spiritual endeavors.

- *What do you value in your personal space and general environment?* Examples can include having a clean home, fresh air, jazz music, being able to walk barefoot on the grass, and sleeping on soft, comfortable bed linens that have a super-high thread count.

- *How do you define your financial values?* Examples of core financial values include living within your means, having financial security for yourself and your family, and sharing wealth with others.

3. Study Your List of Core Values. As you do this, be honest with yourself. Don't worry about how it sounds or if you feel self-conscious, embarrassed, or guilty about listing material items. If you happen to love your Marc Jacobs bag, it's okay to admit this. Simply observe that you appreciate quality craftsmanship or unique designs. Or, maybe you value luxury items, and it signals that you care about having enough money to afford nice things.

Examine the values you have written down, and with each item, ask yourself, *Why is this important to me? What will this bring to my life?* For example, you might have written down that you want to be rich. Why do you want this? What meaning does it hold for you? You might answer that having money makes you feel safe. Ask yourself where this idea came from. Was this a message you got from your parents? Is the notion of financial security truly yours, or did you inherit it?

By deepening your self-inquiry, you will learn so much about what you truly care about, why you care about those values, and where your motivations are coming from. Give expression to all your feelings; don't try to suppress anything. Remember, there are no right or wrong values, only ones that hold meaning for you or not.

4. Narrow Down Your Core Values. Look at all your values. I know these are all important to you, but just as Lacy had to, I want you to set aside five values that aren't at the top of your priority list right now. After you've done that, remove another five. Then another five. Keep going until you are left with five to seven core values.

5. Create Your Core Values Statement. Once you have your core values, write them down in a document or journal, and briefly explain why each value is vital to you. Keep each statement as short as possible so you can easily understand it. An example could be: "I value communication because it minimizes misunderstandings and opens the way for family harmony." After you document the list, it forms a Core Values Statement that you can type up and place somewhere visible.

By aligning your choices and actions with your core values as closely as possible, you are fulfilling your true purpose and manifesting conscious wealth.

No One Plans to Fail, but Many Fail to Plan

David takes such good care of his health that at his last checkup, his doctor said, "I'll see you next year." David, who was 95 years old, didn't take the news well. He was petrified. He had run out of money and was destitute. He dreaded the conversation he would have to have with his son and daughter, who were both nearing retirement age themselves. He would have to ask them for financial support. David never expected to live this long and didn't know where else to turn. While his son and daughter weren't thrilled to hear about their father's lack of planning, they were happy he was still healthy, and they made adjustments to their own plans in order to help him with his ongoing expenses.

David's life did not turn out as he had hoped. It seldom does. I think you would agree that nobody actually sets out to be a burden on their loved ones, run their business into the ground, dissolve their marriage, or get seriously ill and incur huge medical expenses. But disasters happen, and unforeseen events can surprise you sometimes. My recommendation is this: Hope for the best, but plan for the worst.

You don't need to wait for a wake-up call or one of what I call the "5 Ds"—*Death, Disability, Disease, Divorce,* and *Destitution*—in order to start planning. Instead, take the time to assess your values, go after your dreams, and plan accordingly.

Why wait until you lose it all? You don't need to go through a near-death experience to appreciate how valuable your life is or grieve the death of a loved one to appreciate the time you have with family now. If you're willing to change your diet after a diagnosis, if you're willing to treat your partner better after the threat of divorce, if you're willing to tighten your purse strings once you've had a brush with homelessness, why wait? Align with your divine today!

If I had known David when he was a young man, I would have suggested that he dream. *Dream big.* And so should you, regardless of your current age. Dream that you're going to live to be 110, and that your children will go to college, and that you can earn money doing work that you love and be financially free. Imagine the possibilities. Don't limit yourself to what you think can or cannot happen.

If you want a life of abundance, you must stretch your imagination. Be aware of your inner critic who may whisper, "Don't be so selfish," or "You'll never get that." Tune that out and simply ask yourself repeatedly: *What do I want?*

What Do You Want?

It's quite the question: What do *you* want? A surprising number of people have tremendous difficulty answering this. Maybe you aren't used to being asked about your desires. Maybe you focus so much on giving others what they want that you never give yourself the opportunity to determine what *you* want. It's easy to forget about yourself in today's hectic world, but when you're always busy juggling demands, twisting and bending to make everyone else happy, you slip out of alignment and can lose sight of what truly makes *you* happy.

I advise you to be kind to yourself and respect the desires in your heart. You have the power to create abundance, and it's up to you to define what that means. Just as you came up with your core values earlier, you can continue to inquire within to get at your root intentions and goals. The Setting Your Intentions and Goals exercise, which you will find at the close of this step, will help you do this. Whether you intend to feel secure with money or health, or to cherish time and memories with loved ones, or to grow personally and spiritually, as long as your goals are for the highest good, you have every right to achieve them.

Holistic guru Deepak Chopra defines *intention* as the "creative power that fulfills all of our needs, whether for money, relationships, spiritual awakening, or love." When you pray about, meditate on, or journal your deepest intentions, you activate the energetic forces around you and set the wheels in motion for your dreams to manifest. The more awareness you bring to your intentions, the more you will make the right choices and act in accordance with them.

Crystallize Your Intentions into Goals

One of my intentions has been to become more physically fit. I can envision looking leaner, with more muscle tone, strength, and energy. I want to be healthy so I can enjoy a long life with my children and their children. But I need to shift from living in my dreams to actualizing them. To do that, I start with intentions focused on *what* I want and then set goals for *how* I will transform my reality.

My intention to get in shape comes more alive once I set the goal of attending fitness classes three mornings a week over the next three months. A related goal would be to eat healthier, specifically to lower my sugar consumption and increase the number of dark, leafy greens in my diet. By setting these sorts of goals, I build a road map that I can follow to live the life I want.

In order to maximize the effectiveness of your goals, consider writing them in SMART terms: *specific, measurable, actionable, realistic,* and *time-bound.*[2] Achieving financial security is a great intention, but it's too broad to be a goal. Inquire deeper to uncover what financial security looks like for you specifically. Does it mean being out of debt? Or perhaps earning enough money to cover your bills? Or having saved enough to generate an annual income stream of $20,000 a year or $100,000 a year?

A specific goal could be paying off credit-card debt. This is specific and measurable, meaning you will *know* when your balance is at zero. To make this goal actionable, you might aim to pay $200 per month toward your debt. This may or may not be realistic depending on your circumstances. Try to set the goal high, but not so high that it's unrealistic. Only you can decide exactly how much you will pay off each month. Then figure out when you will achieve your goal.

Setting a deadline can motivate you to work toward your goal, as long as you don't let the time frame stress you out. After you've come up with your due date, focus on what you are doing. People can get bogged down by a looming deadline, and this can cause them to feel paralyzed.

Even if you don't make your target contribution each month, you can still do your best to make a partial payment. As for the goal of becoming more physically fit, maybe once in a while you can't get to the gym, but you could still take a walk or dance around to your favorite cardio music after dinner. Just keep trying. You will still be much closer to your dream than if you had done nothing at all.

Meeting Your Financial Goals

Following a map may not guarantee that you will reach your destination, but you'll get closer with it than without it. When I develop holistic financial plans for my clients, I start by asking about what they care about and what they want out of life. For clients who identify saving for retirement as their main priority, we establish their retirement goals by discussing how they would like to spend their time during retirement, when they would like to retire, and how much they are willing to save now in order to achieve that. Although we can analyze all the financial data, clients understand that their retirement can be a moving target since a lot depends on the stability of their income, what the stock markets do, and the inflation and tax rates, as well as their health and lifestyle in the future. Some may wonder, why bother planning given all the unknowns?

No one can control the future. But you have full control over what you do. Don't give up due to uncertainty about the future. I highly encourage you to start taking action today with the mind-set that you *can* achieve your goals, and if the goal line moves, you can adjust.

Another financial goal people put off due to scarcity thinking is saving for college. Common concerns I hear include "What if my kids don't go to college?" and "What if I save too much?" and "What if these accounts get taxed in the future?"

I agree that we don't know what the tax situation or the cost of tuition will be, let alone what our children's futures will be like. There are many unknowns. But if you don't plan for it, retirement or sending your children to college may not even be an option.

Plan as if your kids will go to college and as if you will live long in retirement. The earlier you put things in motion, the more financial and emotional security you will eventually have no matter what happens.

The questions I pose to you are: What if your dreams can come true? Or your child does get into that expensive school? Staying in the Abundance Loop is about having a positive mind-set to make the best choices and taking appropriate actions to align with what you want today.

EXERCISE:
Setting Your Intentions and Goals

Setting an intention is critical. Time waits for no one, and it's so easy to get caught up in reactive mode, putting out your own fires as well as those of others. But imagine what your life could be like if you knew what you wanted and went for it. How wonderful if you could just get done what you wanted . . . *actually done.*

Well, that's the purpose of this exercise. The following suggestions will help you to verify that your intentions are in line with what holds the most meaning for you, specifically the core values that you identified in the previous exercise.

Once you determine what you want, chunk it down into a series of small goals. This process works because when you focus your energy on small, discrete tasks, you feel your progress and are motivated to keep going, creating healthy habits that will eventually manifest your vision.

1. Find a quiet place to breathe and ground yourself. That's right—we're doing it again. The more you practice being in stillness and bringing your awareness to the present, the more likely aligning with your divine becomes a habit. Follow the mindfulness steps that work best for you (from the options presented in Step 2), or just take a few deep breaths and visualize yourself feeling calm and at peace. Visualize yourself connected to the earth, rooted to the ground, like a tree.

2. Keeping your mind clear and calm, write down a list of intentions. Write these in the present tense as if you have already manifested your vision. For example, "I am a best-selling author," as opposed to "I want to be" or "I will be." Bring what you want to achieve in the future into the present.

3. Give thanks for what you have yet to manifest as if you already have manifested it. For example, "I am thankful that I am financially free."

4. Compare this list with your Core Values Statement from the previous exercise. Are they in alignment? If not, try to adjust your intentions to more closely reflect what truly matters to you.

5. Now you are ready to establish some goals to help you manifest your intentions into reality. Remember to follow the SMART acronym: *specific, measurable, actionable, realistic,* and *time-bound.*

6. Create a chart with two columns. In the first column, state your values-based intention. In the second column, think of different tasks required to actualize your intention and formulate SMART goals.

7. If you aren't sure what to do at the beginning or at some point in the process, list as your task the specific research you could do to find out the answers (such as looking up services you need online, visiting your bank or financial planner, or calling someone to gather information).

8. Celebrate the accomplishment of each task, even if it seems small at first, and be grateful for any and all help you receive along the way. Cross each task off your chart as you complete it, and then begin the next task. If something doesn't work out, that's okay. Just adjust your list and try a new path to the same end. Be confident that you can ground yourself anytime and access your Divine Self to guide you whenever you need direction.

An example of an intention and goal-setting list is below. You can add a third column to be able to record your progress and any other notes related to these goals.

Intentions	SMART Goals
I am debt-free.	• Eliminate $10,000 credit-card debt within two years. • Pay down $500 every month on credit-card bills.
I am retired at 70 with $1 million in the bank.	• Cut back on expenses by $200 per month. • Contribute $250 per month into an investment portfolio. • Invest half my tax refund and bonus next spring.
I am a best-selling author.	• Write a book proposal within the next six months. • Build a following of 5,000 fans this year. • Write every day for 15 minutes.
I am growing spiritually, and I meditate every day.	• Pray or meditate ten minutes every morning. • Find a church, temple, or meditation group to join by next month.
I am happy and grateful for my abundant life.	• Write down three blessings in my abundance journal daily. • Practice mindfulness throughout the day.

Key Messages about Clarifying Your Values and Intentions

- Clarifying your values gives you a solid foundation to make sound decisions that result in a meaningful life.

- Intentions are what you want. Goals are how you transform them into reality.

- Hope for the best, but plan for the worst.

- Set clear financial goals and save consistently, without letting fear and uncertainty hinder you from investing in your dreams.

- The more your life reflects your core values, the more abundance you experience.

STEP 5

Calculate Your Resources

Spending money without knowing how much you have or how much you owe is like stumbling in a dark hallway, where you can't see where you're going and could potentially fall down the stairs. It's time to flip that light switch on and proceed with confidence. Clarity enables you to exercise your power to make conscious choices and take deliberate action.

Here in Step 5 is your chance to sum up and interpret both your financial and your spiritual wealth. I will walk you through preparing a financial balance sheet that will look at your total net worth in monetary terms. Then you'll be asked to complete a spiritual balance sheet, to take an inventory of your self-worth as measured by your values. You will then look at your cash flow and energy flow and assess what is going on so you can make the best decisions to get yourself on the right track to achieving your goals.

All I ask is that you proceed with faith that you can move past your fears and experience gratitude for the knowledge, no matter what the results are. I want you to feel empowered to reclaim your abundance, which is your natural birthright.

Please know that I tried hard to simplify my language instead of using the kind of financial jargon that tends to scare people. It's important to me that you feel as comfortable as possible in the process of assuming responsibility for your financial future. It is my intention to show you the connection between the Scarcity Loop and the Abundance Loop in both financial and spiritual terms.

What Is a Financial Balance Sheet?

Corporations use financial statements to track how much cash they have, how it is spent, and how much they owe. As you create your own financial statement, you'll gain this same knowledge about yourself.

Your balance sheet is a snapshot of your current financial health. It consists of two basic lists: One shows what you have, including cash, investments, real estate, cars, or anything that has immediate cash value. These are your assets. The other shows what you owe, including your credit-card debt, your mortgage, and any other loans. These are your liabilities. When you subtract your debt from your assets, the difference is your net worth.

The equation looks like this:

Assets – Liabilities = Net Worth

Although this figure tells you where you stand at this point, the real value comes when you track your net worth over time and evaluate whether you are operating in the Abundance Loop or the Scarcity Loop. A sound financial choice, such as saving, investing, or lowering debt, increases your net worth. A poor choice, such as racking up too much consumer debt, decreases your net worth.

Regardless of where you stand today, you can take conscious action to improve your net worth. For now, let's capture your baseline in the following exercise.

EXERCISE:
Create Your Financial Balance Sheet

It's time to create your own balance sheet, and I believe you'll be glad you did. Read how to do this exercise, then set aside several hours, or even several days, to do this—it's that important. You might need more time if your financial records are hard to locate.

1. Collect all your financial records such as checking account, savings account, retirement accounts, college-savings accounts, brokerage accounts, and so on. This is also a great opportunity to track down those old 401(k)s that you may have left behind with past employers and consolidate them into a single Rollover IRA where you can monitor the investments more carefully. You can get a rough estimate of your home on Zillow.com and find the value of your car with Kelley Blue Book.

    Regarding your liabilities, pull up your credit-card statements, your mortgage statement, and your student loans and other loan documents. Be sure to also include any loans outstanding to your family or friends, assuming you intend to pay them back.

2. Now that you've gathered all your data, open your own blank copy of a financial balance sheet (any financial or spreadsheet software will do), or just draw one in your journal to look similar to the chart on the next page.

3. List each asset and its current market value, which is how much the investment account or property is worth today. Add up all your assets and jot that figure down under Total Assets.

4. List each liability and the outstanding balances. Total up your liabilities.

5. Subtract your total liabilities from your total assets, and note your net worth.

6. Breathe. You did it! Take a moment to appreciate all that you just accomplished in organizing your data and taking steps to become financially healthy!

Financial Balance Sheet (also called Your Net Worth Statement)	
<u>Assets</u> **What You Have**	<u>Liabilities</u> **What You Owe**
Home Value:	Mortgage Balance:
Car Value:	Car Balance:
Savings:	Student-Loan Balance:
Checking:	Credit-Card #1 Balance:
Investments:	Credit-Card #2 Balance:
IRA/Roth IRA:	Credit-Card #3 Balance:
401(k):	Other Loan Balance:
Employee Stock:	Debt to Family or Others:
College Savings:	Consolidation Loan Balance:
Other Assets:	Other Liabilities:
Total Assets:	Total Liabilities:
	Net Worth: (Net Worth = Assets – Liabilities)

Understanding Your Financial Balance Sheet

Whether your net worth is in the millions or down in negative territory, this figure is simply that—a figure. Your personal balance sheet takes a snapshot of your finances in a moment in time, and every day those numbers change. Your paycheck hits, you pay bills, you charge dinner on your credit card . . . you get the picture.

As unpleasant as all this analysis might be, it's vitally important to uncover the truth of your financial habits. Many women have confided in me that they are so afraid of dealing with money that they don't even open their bank and investment statements. Some say they are terribly afraid to talk to their husband or partner about money. These anxiety-driven choices to ignore your finances just heighten your fears, entrapping you once again in the Scarcity Loop.

So in summary, no matter what your financial balance sheet reveals about your net worth, take personal pride in knowing you just took a brave and important step toward understanding your own situation. I applaud your courage and commitment in uncovering your own financial truth. And you know from the first steps in this book that you are so much more than your net worth, and that is where we are going next.

What Is a Spiritual Balance Sheet?

The financial balance sheet is clear-cut: *What you have minus what you owe equals your net worth.* However, this doesn't determine your true worth. Regardless of your net worth, your self-worth is completely separate, and it's determined by how you value yourself.

You cannot objectively measure your self-worth. No one can. Your spiritual worth cannot be evaluated by anyone else, even though many might try. Maybe you had parents who constantly undermined your value, or you have friends or partners who belittle you. Nevertheless, it is up to you to accept or reject any of these opinions of your worth. This is why it is called *self-worth*. You, and only you, determine your own worth. Everyone else's opinion of you is just that, an *opinion*. Unless you choose to believe their opinion, it has no bearing on the value you place on yourself.

In this next exercise, I challenge you to question any negative beliefs you hold about yourself and encourage you to think about what you appreciate about yourself. Very few people feel comfortable praising themselves. If you find yourself struggling with this, try collating any job recommendations people have written for you in the past, birthday cards, Facebook posts, or other loving written tributes, as well as anything else you have that shows you are appreciated by others. It will help you take stock of your spiritual assets.

EXERCISE:
Create Your Spiritual Balance Sheet

This exercise will help you create your own spiritual balance sheet so you can assess your self-worth. As shown, the table will have two columns just like your financial balance sheet: "Assets" and "Liabilities." But because only you can determine your own value, your spiritual assets and liabilities are based on your beliefs about yourself. Your assets are positive beliefs you hold about yourself, and your liabilities are negative beliefs about yourself. I've listed some prompts to help you get started, but don't feel you must follow them.

1. I encourage you to take out your journal or laptop, and create a table with two columns.

2. In the assets column, list all the qualities you like about yourself. What do you believe are your positive traits? What characteristics are you proud of? What do you love about yourself and feel grateful for? What do your friends love about you? If you're not sure, ask them!

3. Take a deep breath, and reflect on the list you just wrote down. How do you feel about yourself?

4. Now let's look at your negative beliefs, your spiritual liabilities. List the aspects of yourself you don't feel proud of. What do you believe you aren't enough of? What do you try to avoid dealing with because it causes too much discomfort? Once you complete this step, you might end up with a ridiculously long list of negative beliefs about yourself. However, the next part of this exercise will help you determine if these so-called negative traits really matter. Simply having a long list of spiritual assets or liabilities doesn't determine your self-worth. What matters is how important these characteristics are to you. Again, let's refer back to your list of core values.

5. Circle any of the characteristics that reflect your core values, whether they fall on the positive or negative side. For instance, maybe you are proud of how funny you can be, and one of your core values is humor—circle it. Maybe you value punctuality, but you (and your friends) hate that you are always late—circle it.

6. Mark a "+1" next to the circled assets that are in line with your values.

7. Mark a "−1" next to the circled liabilities that signal a disconnect with your values.

8. Now total the assets and liabilities that you have marked with a +1 or a −1. The result will be your self-worth number. This figure indicates how you feel about yourself at this point in time. After the chart, I have included more information about how to understand this unique balance sheet and recommendations to raise your self-worth.

Your Spiritual Balance Sheet (also called Your Self-Worth Statement)	
Assets **Positive Beliefs about Self**	Liabilities **Negative Beliefs about Self**
My positive traits:	My negative traits:
I have confidence in my ability to:	I lack confidence in my ability to:
I am proud of:	I am ashamed of:
People love that I am:	People say I should be more:
I am glad I am:	I wish I were more:
I am at peace that I am:	I am bothered that I am:
I am grateful that I am:	I fear that I am:
Total Circled Assets:	*Total Circled Liabilities:*
	Self-Worth:

Understanding Your Spiritual Balance Sheet

If your self-worth total is a positive number, you will likely feel pretty good about yourself because your life reflects what you care about. If you have a net negative number, you might feel disappointed or concerned that your life isn't necessarily in sync with what you value.

Please don't fret if this is the case. The point of this exercise is not to walk away with a positive or negative number, but to become aware of how you think about yourself and gauge if you are behaving and making decisions in accordance with what you truly care about. Bravo for getting to this point!

But there's more. Take your time and address one of the circled liabilities that you desperately want to change in your life. Can you set an intention and some discrete action steps to turn that particular spiritual liability into an asset? For example, let's say you believed that you weren't a good enough mother, and because one of your core values is time with family, you marked a "–1" next to this liability. Turn any shame and frustration that comes from your belief that you are not a good mother into a catalyst for change. Set a positive intention such as, *I am a caring mother and spend quality time reading to or playing with my son.* Write this down, say it to yourself repeatedly, and consciously make the time to be with him. Check in with yourself regularly to see if your actions are aligning with your intention.

Once you've done this, cross out the negative belief in your liabilities column, and write it in the assets column as a positive belief about yourself: *I am a present mother, and I am doing enough for my son.* You then shift into the Abundance Loop: Your gratitude for being a good enough mother allows you to peacefully read or play with your child, forging a stronger bond.

Remember, you are enough just as you are in this very moment. As your life unfolds, you can actively make choices that better reflect your core values.

When your life reflects what matters to you, it doesn't matter what others say. You have set your own benchmark, and you measure your own progress.

Your Self-Worth Transcends Your Net Worth

If your self-worth is intact, you are abundant and can create the space for more abundance to flow into your life. Positive self-worth is, in many ways, your most precious resource.

A balance sheet is used to help clarify the net financial value of what you have, but as we've discussed, what you have does not equate to who you are. Your house, car, clothes, electronics, and other possessions are not "you"; they simply represent stuff that you spent money on (whether with cash or credit) to make your life easier and to make yourself feel safe, secure, and happy. A large investment portfolio may bring you peace of mind and allow you the freedom to do what you want, but the money does not define you.

Also remember that your net worth doesn't equal your self-worth. You could own ten mansions, each containing every luxury item possible, and be at the top of the Forbes list of billionaires, and still feel empty inside. Others may be in awe of you, but you could still question what you are really worth.

Why do we work so hard to build our fortunes? What's it all for? What do the fancy cars, clothes, and gadgets really get us? In the end, we acquire things to feel that we are worthy, deserving of love. Deep down every single one of us wants to feel loved. And unconsciously many people believe that by having a lot of stuff, they will be loved. Getting new stuff may boost your happiness, but only temporarily. Research shows that after a certain number of years, and no matter how much stuff we have, we all fall back to our baseline level of happiness. We may get more stuff, and more after that, but we will always end up at our baseline.

But something does endure, and let me share what that is: *love*. When you love yourself, when you realize how much you are truly worth, when you realize how lovable you are, you will fall in love with *you*. You will finally see your true worth. You will appreciate your unique and critical being. You are a part of this universe, which would not be the same without you. Your essence is worth far more than the dollars sitting in your investment portfolio or the possessions in your closet. Your self-worth is substantial even if you have no money and are unemployed. Your self-worth is priceless.

No End to Seeking External Validation

We all know how easy it is to get caught up in the hustle and bustle of everyday activities. When you've spent a full workday putting out fires, you want the rest of your day to be easy. With access to easy credit, it's tempting to eat in expensive restaurants and to shop for items that promise to make your life more convenient. But living this way may keep you entrapped in the Scarcity Loop, whether or not you are conscious of this happening. Living in abundance doesn't mean "having" everything you could ever want; it means understanding your own personal preferences, honoring your own core values, and living from your Divine Self and no longer from your ego.

Furthermore, if you spend irresponsibly, you are stuck in the Scarcity Loop even if you own many things. If you've overspent, when your credit card and other bills arrive you may end up feeling exhausted, guilty, or ashamed. You may be unable to pay your bills, which, in turn, will trigger late fees and balloon your debt even more. Living within your means, and in alignment with a financial and spiritual plan, is a way to move forward and live in abundance.

Save and Spend Consciously

You have the power to choose how you save and spend your time, money, and energy. In order to start building your wealth, you first need to get clarity about what is going on today. One excellent way to get this clarity is to figure out how much money you have coming in and how much is going out.

In the past, I resisted tracking my money because I hated feeling guilty and constrained. But living in ignorance was keeping me stuck in the Scarcity Loop. I had to make a conscious choice to stop resisting my fears and face my financial truth. I eased my way into it by taking a deep breath and telling myself (even if I didn't fully believe it at the time): *I'm grateful for the awareness of how much I have spent and how much I have left.* By shifting from fear to gratitude about my cash flow, I was able to transform my relationship to money.

Financial clarity allows me to relax and reminds me that I'm in control of where my money is going. Tracking my income and expenses has become a time of empowering myself and getting clear about my wealth, regardless of the amount. It's akin to tracking my weight. I step on the scale every morning and gain information that tells me how I'm doing.

Let's start by tracking where your money goes, and then we can assess how much you actually need. We will prepare a Cash Flow Statement to help us with this task. In basic terms, a Cash Flow Statement tracks where your dollars are going. Your *cash flow* is calculated by subtracting your total outflows from your total inflows.

Money In – Money Out = Cash Flow

If you have more money coming in than going out, you have positive cash flow. The basis of building financial wealth is having positive cash flow so you can add to your assets and increase your net worth. Too many people expect the stock markets to do the heavy lifting, or they expect a big payday, or to land their dream job with a fat salary. But I have witnessed people with modest incomes retire as millionaires because they had positive cash flow, and they were able to save and invest on a regular basis.

On the flip side, when you spend more money than you have coming in, you have negative cash flow, which is a drain on your resources. Dipping into savings regularly to pay for an overly expensive lifestyle dwindles your asset base, which otherwise could be growing. If you rely on credit cards to fund your lifestyle, mounting debt will eventually debilitate you, preventing you from living the life you really want down the line. Instant gratification may soothe your ego, but it will eventually jeopardize your financial future.

EXERCISE:
Create Your Cash Flow Statement

The following exercise is quite detailed but really important. You already gathered your financial statements to create your balance sheet; however, please check if you have your income and expense information, as well, from banks and credit cards. You want to collect information that will help you determine where your money is going. Remember that the cash you spend buying coffee is as relevant an expense as the money you spend for rent or your mortgage. You need to accurately figure out how much money you have coming in and going out. If you already track your money in Quicken or through Mint.com, bravo!

Begin by looking at the sample Cash Flow Statement below, which is organized into two parts. On the left side, list all your money flowing in. Income sources could include your salary, bonus, unemployment, alimony, child support, social security, disability income, rental income, retirement income, and investment income. List how much you receive from each source and break it down by month.

Now work on the right side of your Cash Flow Statement. List the money flowing out, which are all your expenses. Start with your monthly debt payments such as mortgage, car, and student loans; and move on to other regular expenses such as child care, phone, utilities, insurance, food, and so on. Remember to go through all your receipts and look at things like your credit-card statements to see how much you spend on gas, groceries, restaurants, utilities, gym membership, and random shopping.

The goal here isn't just to protect you from financial disasters. I want to see you thrive. I want you to create financial security for yourself so you can live the life you want. The key to financial security is positive cash flow. Essentially, when you have more money coming in than going out, you have positive cash flow, which can be added to your savings. Otherwise, you will deplete your savings to fund your lifestyle, and over time, this will ultimately lead to scarcity.

Your Cash Flow Statement	
Incoming	**Outgoing**
Salary, Wages:	Home (rent/mortgage, HOA dues, property taxes, insurance, maintenance):
Social Security:	Automobile (payments, insurance, gas, maintenance):
Interest, Dividends from Investments:	Food (groceries, eating out):
Child Support:	Utilities (electricity, water, garbage, cable, Internet, phone):
Alimony:	Medical (doctors, treatments, insurance, medication):
Disability:	Shopping (clothes, electronics, appliances):
Trust:	Leisure (gym, club, travel, entertainment):
Annuity:	Child Care (education, babysitting, activities):
Rental Income:	Additional Debt Payments (not including what you add to your credit card every month):
Total inflows:	**Total outflows:**

EXERCISE:
Understanding Budgeting Basics

Congratulations on collecting all the information to see if your household is operating in the black or in the red. Now that you've calculated your cash flow, it's the perfect time to take the next logical step and create a budget. A budget is a great way to help you figure out how much you need to meet your lifestyle expenses and your goals.

While your Cash Flow Statement helps you see where you spent your money in the past, a budget helps you see how much you need for the future. It's a planning tool that helps you clarity what you can afford to do and how much in extra resources you need.

There are multiple ways to do this. Budgeting apps and online calculators are available for free. Or you can create your own spreadsheet, or simply use your journal. It doesn't matter what you use. The key is to use it consistently, on a regular basis.

Refer to past bills for things like utilities, taxes, and other expenses; and estimate the next 12 months based on them. For all your expenses, break each of them down into monthly amounts. For instance, if you pay your property taxes every six months, divide your bill by six to get to your monthly figure.

Remember, if you plan to make minimum payments each month against specific loans or credit cards to bring down your level of debt over the next year, those amounts have to be included in your budget process. Likewise, if you plan to save a certain amount per month, take that into consideration.

Once you've filled in the full chart, track how you are doing on a monthly basis against it. Monitoring your progress will empower you to make better decisions about how to allocate your money. The more you can stay within your budget—or better yet, under it—the more you have to save and invest. Step 6 covers more details on building your wealth.

This budget process is an essential tool to achieve your desired financial well-being and to help you plan for major expenses that might be once in a lifetime, like a wedding, sending your child to college, or taking an extended vacation overseas. Estimate all the costs well in advance and work out a plan for how you will pay for everything.

Likewise, if you intend to quit your job and start your own business, you must calculate the minimum amount of income you need to cover your living expenses until the business gets off the ground. If you are planning to retire, your annual lifestyle costs will greatly influence when you can afford to do so. The less you need to live, the sooner you can retire. Again, more details about planning for retirement are in Step 6.

Budget		
	Monthly	**Annually**
Mortgage/Rent		
Property Taxes		
Home Insurance		
HOA Fees		
Home Maintenance		
Car Payment		
Auto Insurance		
Gas		

	Monthly	Annually
Car Maintenance		
Utilities		
Cell Phone		
Child Care		
Tuition/Camps		
Lessons		
Medical		
Dental		
Vision		
Groceries		
Eating Out		
Clothes		
Toys		
Gym		
Sports		
Personal Grooming		
Pets		
Entertainment		
Electronics		
Laundry/Dry Cleaning		
Vacation		
Hobbies		
Gifts		
Miscellaneous		
Student-Loan Payments		
Other Loan Payments		
Charity		
Retirement Savings		
Education Savings		
Other Savings		
Total Lifestyle:		

Where Is Your Energy Going?

While it's important to develop financial awareness and track where your money is going, it is equally important—in some ways even *more* vital—for you to track where you spend your time and energy. You can almost always get more money if you must. But there's only so much time you are given. You get the same 24 hours a day that everyone else does. How do you spend your day? How do you *want* to spend it?

Besides time, your energy is also finite. I mean the personal energy inside, the vitality you use throughout the day. When your energy inflow is greater than your energy outflow, you create a positive energy flow, which is critical for sustaining your health and well-being.

But when you deplete your energy at a faster rate than you renew it, you operate at a deficit—and that can lead to major stress and health problems. It doesn't matter how much money you earn or save; if you don't have the energy to enjoy the fruits of your labor, what's the point?

Do you want to simply pass the time or make the most of your life doing things you enjoy with people you love? Assuming that you want the latter (or else you wouldn't have gotten this far in the book), I've created two exercises here to help you track and increase your energy flow.

First is your Energy Flow Statement, which is designed to heighten your awareness about what fuels you and what drains you. The second exercise helps you track how you spend your energy and to calculate if you are left feeling "ahhhh" or "ugghh" at the end of the day.

EXERCISE:
Create Your Energy Flow Statement

You will need about an hour to do this exercise. Use this time to think about how you spend your days, weeks, months, and years. Consider browsing your old calendars and diaries to see how you spent your time and energy in the past.

In order to create your own chart, take out your journal or laptop. Begin by looking at the sample Energy Flow Statement below. On the left-hand side, list all the activities that boost your joy and energy. I've given you some prompts to help you. You can also list time spent with people or organizations that make you feel better. Try answering the prompts with complete honesty.

Then on the right-hand side, list all the activities that seem to deplete you, bring you down, or waste your time. Follow the prompts or enter your own ideas.

Now, indicate the number of minutes (20, 60, 90, or more) that you spend on average each day on each of the activities, people, and things in both columns. Be aware that it's not so much the grand totals that you need to pay attention to. This exercise is intended to help you see where your precious time and energy are going.

This new knowledge will enable you to begin to make better use of your time by decreasing the energy sappers and replacing them with energy boosters. The next exercise in a few pages will build on this concept and help you realize how your daily activities (where you spend your energy) relate to your core values.

Your Energy Flow Statement	
Ahhhh. *Energy Boosters*	*Ugghh.* *Energy Sappers*
People who support me:	People who stress me:
Activities that excite me:	Activities that I dread doing:

Eating habits that fuel me:	Eating habits that leave me sluggish:
Thoughts that make me happy:	Thoughts that evoke anxiety:
What motivates me at work:	What stresses me at work:
Environment that enlivens me:	Environment that frustrates me:
Volunteer commitments that excite me:	Volunteer commitments that drain me:
Small things that recharge me:	Small things that deplete me:
Interactions that energize me:	Interactions that drain me:
Spiritual practices that renew me:	Practices that bring me down:
Emotions that uplift me:	Emotions that upset me:

Understanding Your Energy Flow Statement

Look at what you filled out and reread each comment you added. Notice how even just thinking about that person, activity, or interaction makes you feel. The more you can be aware of your thoughts and feelings, the more you get in touch with your authentic self. When you practice mindfulness and align with your true self, you will feel more at peace. On the other hand, when you are running around and feel obligated or forced to deal with people or things that you don't want to, it creates tension and drains you.

Emotions that arise from joy, gratitude, abundance, kindness, generosity, love, and forgiveness can bring you greater peace and a sense of renewal. Conversely, emotions such as jealousy, anger, resentment, hatred, frustration, sadness, and fear can weigh you down and suck you bone-dry.

The ultimate goal is to be conscious of how you are feeling throughout the day and take actions that align with your Divine Self. Time doesn't drag when you are deeply engaged and loving what you do. When you're excited about your daily activities, you go the extra mile and perform at peak levels. You feel at one with your Divine Self and manifest conscious wealth.

So why should you take a job that doesn't fulfill you and causes you to spend your precious time fulfilling other people's obligations, trying to make other people happy? Instead, commit yourself to creating abundance in your life and be willing to advocate for yourself. Stand up for what you believe in, and invest your time, money, and energy in whatever will enrich your happiness. By honoring what you truly care about and spending time with people who uplift you, you will be energized to work productively and experience true wealth.

EXERCISE:
Tracking Your Alignment

You feel abundant when your life reflects what you most care about. In this exercise, we will look at the level of congruency between the way you spend your time and money and your core values. For example, spending time and money at the gym may align with the value of optimal health. However, strolling through the mall or watching television may be regular habits, but they may not align with any of your core values.

Be aware that feelings of shame or guilt, thoughts of *I shouldn't be wasting my time on that,* or some other "shoulds" may come up. When they do, keep telling yourself that those criticisms are just your ego talking. Tune out that chatter and focus on completing this activity honestly from your own heart, because that is how you will ultimately determine how to use your resources to manifest the life you want.

- Start by taking a mental rundown of your average day and think about how you spend your time and money. Write down a full list of everything you spend time and money on, and include activities such as shopping, dining out, and driving or sitting in transit.

- Ask yourself what core value each of these activities or purchases reflects. It's okay if they don't align with any of your values. This exercise is meant to sift those out.

- Now refer to the chart below to better understand which uses of your time and money are in alignment and which aren't.

Congruency Check		
	Misalignment	**Alignment**
Time	How do you spend your time in misalignment with your core values?	How do you spend your time in alignment with your core values?
Money	What do you spend your money on that misaligns with your core values?	What do you spend your money on that aligns with your core values?

If you already are spending most of your time and money in ways that are meaningful to you, congratulations! If not, consider scaling back on resources spent on activities and purchases are that not in alignment with your core values. By identifying the misalignments, you can see the importance of consciously choosing to do things or buy things that will make you feel more fulfilled.

Now that you have gained clarity about what you want from Step 4 and calculated where you stand both financially and energetically from Step 5, you are ready to take action. In the next step, you will learn specifically what is required to achieve your goals and track your progress toward your divine abundance.

Key Messages about Calculating Your Resources

- Calculate your resources to help you manifest your abundance, which is your natural birthright.

- Your financial balance sheet measures your net worth by the amount of assets you have.

- Your spiritual balance sheet measures your self-worth by your core values.

- Manage your budget in order to maintain positive cash flow, so you can save and invest.

- Spend time with people and activities that boost your energy level.

- Eliminate time spent doing things that sap your energy.

STEP 6

Commit to Conscious Action

If you want your dreams to come true, you must be willing to take action. You know in your heart this is true, but how often do you put off getting started on a major personal project or initiative? Even if you really, really want it, there are always other things to do with your time, and I know that big decisions can be daunting. As a result, some people continue to wallow in indecision forever and never actually get anywhere.

Take the example of two co-workers I heard about who expressed interest in participating in a missionary project overseas, helping to build orphanages in Africa. Frank and Joseph both worked at IT jobs in Boston and heard about the project through another friend. They talked all the time about how exciting it would be to do it—a once-in-a-lifetime experience.

Then one September, they agreed to go the following June. It was going to be a six-month placement, and they were so excited. Both men attended the mandatory orientation session with the NGO that was organizing the mission. Each received a handbook of instructions to follow to help them get everything done in time to travel on June 1 the following year.

Joseph read the whole handbook immediately and took notes of the many things that had to be done and the deadlines for the paperwork. He found out he had to do things like get clearance from his boss to take a sabbatical; gather three personal letters of reference; fill out a detailed application; get a physical, a doctor's note, and various vaccinations; apply for his passport; arrange for a friend to take his dog for the six months and for someone to watch his apartment . . . the list went on and on.

Each volunteer going on the missionary trip had to pay for his own flight and get international medical coverage, so Joseph made a savings plan to cover all the various expenses. He also realized he needed to arrange for his rent, insurance, and car payments to all be covered while he was out of the country, so he added those things to his list. He found a part-time job tutoring computer students at a nearby high school for four months, to make sure he would have enough money saved to cover everything. He was so thankful that he landed that extra job because it fit his skills perfectly, and he could do it in the evenings.

Frank, on the other hand, only glanced at the handbook and got rather overwhelmed by the detailed instructions and the financial implications. Although Joseph offered to walk him through it, Frank declined and said he would do it in his own way, on his own time. But there were just too many uncertainties and too much organization for Frank to tackle; any time he thought about it, he just kept putting it off. The months passed quickly, and eventually it became clear that Frank had done only a few of the easier things, like getting his passport and looking into the cost of flights.

I think you know how this ends. On June 1, Joseph was fully prepared—mentally, physically, and financially—for the trip of a lifetime, bags packed, and smiling broadly as he waited for his flight. Frank was still at work that day at his job in Boston, with nothing but his passport and a long list of excuses as to why he didn't make it.

What made the difference here? Joseph was deeply grateful for the opportunity and took action, *conscious action,* which allowed him to make his dream come true. Frank let fear, anxiety, and indecision rule the day, and he missed out. Joseph embraced the possibilities of it all, taking daily actions toward it, following his gut, and fully expecting a positive experience. Frank got stuck in scarcity, a loop he was unable to break free from.

Step 6 in the Abundance Loop is about committing to conscious action. Being organized is important, but this chapter is about more than that. Your dreams come true and you experience more abundance when you passionately embrace life. Scarcity doesn't have a chance against people who are fully committed and willing to put themselves first and make their goals the priority. Let me explain how you can be that kind of person.

Different Voice, Different Choice

We all have a choice. What is the voice you choose to listen to? Does it come from your ego or from your Divine Self? By now, you know you can feel the difference. The ego makes you contract while the divine makes you expand. Do you feel you need to hunker down and defend yourself in fear, or can you open up and move with grace? As tiny infants, we all started out the same, yet we have different ways of coping and getting along in life.

Think about babies: Those precious little people in the early stages of ego development express their needs the minute they are born. Hungry, tired, or wet, they liberally communicate when something doesn't feel right. As they develop into toddlers, they start to see themselves as an independent being separate from their caretaker. They eventually recognize they don't have to merge with what their parents want and do (to some parents' dismay).

As babies grow up, they recognize that they actually have a choice. If they don't like something, they yell "No!" and clearly signal their refusal to comply. They grow into unique individuals with their own thoughts and desires. The raw honesty and unhindered questions and actions of children can be so refreshing to witness and elicit deep joy from many adults.

But then as people mature and become aware of negative feedback, they soon learn that expressing their desires might not always be acceptable. What was once natural behavior now becomes a decision point. Can we act a certain way or not? Do we express our thoughts or not? We learn that by conforming, we gain acceptance and love.

Your parents, caretakers, and others in your life meant well in teaching you the proper ways to behave, but the unintended consequence of muting your voice and molding your behaviors was that you suppressed your desires and, sadly, your authentic self. Well, with the power of your awareness you can now commit to reshaping the way you think about yourself and the life you want. I guarantee that as long you feel unworthy, the way Frank did in the opening story, you will make choices that reinforce your feeling of unworthiness. Choose instead to act like Joseph, and you will create abundance. Say yes to a life of prosperity; say yes to the best you. Commit to taking action today.

Job Choice Requires Action

A 2013 Gallup poll revealed that 70 percent of Americans either hate their jobs or are completely disengaged. We all know people who complain about their work, managers, and customers. But when we ask them why they don't take action to get a different job, they often answer, "I can't quit my job. I have no choice. I gotta pay the bills."

Many people feel stuck because they believe they don't have other options, and maybe you have felt this way, or still do. You tell yourself, *I'm not qualified to do anything else, I could never find another job,* or *I have to support my family.* Whatever your reasoning is, it's actually your limited perspective and fear that keep you stuck in a Scarcity Loop and in a job you really can't stand.

Changing jobs may give you some temporary relief, but be aware it might not solve the root problem. Have you ever quit a job you hated only to encounter similar feelings of frustration at the next one? Remember the happiness equation from Step 3 that states that 50 percent of happiness is within your control, of which only 10 percent is derived from your circumstances.

Changing your thoughts and actions affects up to 40 percent of your happiness.

Before jumping ship to a new job, then, first examine your attitudes and beliefs about who you are and your relationship to money. You'll want to make sure your new position and work environment are in alignment with your true self and your core values. That way your new opportunity will turn out to be fulfilling and not just another lousy job.

Every Choice Has Consequences

When your alarm goes off in the morning, you can get out of bed and squeeze in a workout, or hit the snooze button and catch up on some much-needed rest. Both options have benefits, but each leads to a different consequence. Working out may get you closer to your target weight. Extra sleep may be better for your mood.

You can show up 100 percent for your job and be grateful for the opportunities it provides, or you can complain about the salary and the hours. Putting your best foot forward with gratitude is more likely to increase your productivity and your chances for a promotion, whereas spreading your negative attitude will frustrate you further and potentially create a toxic work environment for yourself and others.

These are just a few examples that highlight an undeniable fact: Whether you are aware of your choices or not, each action, reaction, or nonaction you take results in a specific consequence. These outcomes accumulate over time and become your life story. The choices you made in the past led you to where you are today, and the choices you make now shape your future. You might think your talent, skills, money, networking, relationships, or charming personality is what makes you (or will make you) successful. But it's really your choices as to how you leverage your wonderful assets that determine your life.

Your brain and ego might orient you toward fear and caution, but you need to realize that holding on to fear is itself a *choice*—not a good choice, in my opinion, but still a choice you have made. I continue to encourage you to take the other road, free of fear, where you will see your well-being and sense of self-empowerment improve as you make better choices.

The thoughts you hold on to greatly influence your behavior. For instance, fearful thoughts may lead you to take on jobs that leave you underpaid or not living up to your potential because you don't believe in yourself. Or your fear of hurting a sales associate's feelings may lead you to buy clothing you don't really want or need.

When you realize you have enough, and are enough, you'll try to get the job you really want, and that increases the chances that maybe you will get it! You'll stop purchasing things you know you don't need. You might even develop the courage to turn down the friend who continually asks for money and rarely, if ever, ends up paying it back. I wish I had learned that particular lesson sooner, but better late than never. Regardless, I am thankful because now I can spot a mooch a mile away.

Breaking Habits Through Conscious Choice

It's time for a story. Meet Sharon. She loved to treat her friends to lunch. She regularly met up with women from her church or her children's school to go to a cute restaurant. At the end of the fabulous meal, Sharon gladly picked up the check. Grateful that she had plenty of money, she felt good about her ability to afford nice lunches for herself and her friends.

However, after a while, Sharon found herself questioning why her friends rarely made an attempt to reciprocate her generosity. Although she had the financial means to pay, she found herself longing for the experience of being treated to a meal herself. Her frustration and resentment escalated as she started to think that these women might be taking advantage of her.

She wanted to be generous, but saw that she just kept getting hurt. Did Sharon have a choice? Absolutely. But at that point, she was unaware of the power of her thoughts. She identified as a victim, and her thoughts represented this. *The root cause of Sharon's suffering was her underlying belief that she was not worthy of real love.* Sharon's life ran on the rails of her self-commentary: *I'm not worth real love. I don't deserve to be treated well.* It's difficult to stand up for what you want when you feel you don't deserve respect.

Like Sharon, perhaps you also feel that your choices have become such deeply ingrained habits that they don't even feel like choices anymore. Repeating the same patterns keeps you on your current path. You can't expect your life to change until you are willing to change your mind-set and behaviors.

Sharon eventually did take conscious action. She took a year-long break from her friends to focus on her personal growth and to develop a stronger sense of self. She had to hear that she *is enough* over and over again from her husband and her life coach, and she finally began to appreciate her own self-worth. She now knows that she does have a choice in how she views herself and how she acts with her friends.

It turned out that a couple of her friends missed her and she reconciled with them, but now when they eat out, they split the bill fairly. Sharon also found some new people to have lunch with, where they take turns picking different restaurants and picking up the tab, happy to support each other equitably and still have fun.

Doing Nothing Is Still a Choice

I have a friend who has a values conflict many of us can identify with. A corporate sales executive who spent the last 20 years successfully climbing the ranks of a high-tech firm, Cheryl is now married with one child. But she feels burned-out and is itching to do something entrepreneurial that will give her more flexibility with her time and energy. However, she's grown so accustomed to an affluent lifestyle and being able to afford private-school tuition, country-club membership, a summer house on the beach, and annual vacations abroad that she doesn't feel she has any other option but to stay in her current job.

The fact is, though, Cheryl *does* have a choice, and she has made it. She has chosen her lifestyle over personal job satisfaction and work-life balance. Doing nothing about her situation is a choice. She tolerates the daily stress of having to exceed her sales quotas so she can afford to pay for her child's elite education and her family's luxury vacation time.

Then again, she might not need such expensive escapes if she were content in her job. Earning a high salary so you can spend more money doesn't bring happiness, especially if you're truly miserable at work.

Like Cheryl, you may also have made a choice by not leaving a particular situation, job, or relationship. You might hate every minute of it, but, in the end, you have chosen not to fight for something better, something healthier, something that gives you more balance.

If this situation sounds familiar to you, let me say this: Yes, you are an adult; you can do what you want. But you must always pay the consequences. Don't be surprised if one day you break down at work because of mental stress or have to take a leave of absence because of physical pain. You wouldn't be the first person to experience a health crisis because of a misalignment between your work and your core values; actually, it happens quite often. Hopefully you will choose to make the change yourself, rather than have the change forced upon you.

EXERCISE:
How Choices Affect Your Abundance

This is a good time to dive deep and inquire into the choices you are making. This exercise looks at why we make choices and how those choices make us feel. Don't short-change yourself in this process and simply answer, "It feels good." If it does feel good, inquire further. What about the choice makes you feel good? Are you trying to avoid feeling something else; or does it genuinely feel good in body, mind, and soul? How does it impact others? Determine if your daily choices result in the outcome you really want. If they do not, it's time for you to make some better choices.

- How do you choose to spend your time? Is this in line with your core values? Does this bring you the most joy? What are the trade-offs? What else would you rather be doing?

- How do you choose to earn, share, and spend your money? Is it in line with your core values? What are the trade-offs?

- What information do you choose to absorb and retain? How do you feed and calm your mind?

- Whom do you choose to surround yourself with? Why? How do you feel when you hang around these individuals?

- Whom do you choose to hire to take care of your finances, your health, your legal matters, and your spiritual life? Are these individuals aligned with your core values?

Conscious wealth is a result of conscious choices. When your core values guide your decisions, you live with conviction, clarity, and gratitude and you ease into the Abundance Loop. The aggregate of your conscious choices is your abundance.

Action Strategies to Achieve Financial Abundance

Now that you know you can reclaim your power over money and that you no longer have to let your fear of money overpower you, how do you actually become financially wealthy? Well, I like to break it down to three overall things you need to take charge of:

1. Your financial *means;*

2. Your financial *security;* and

3. Your financial *independence.*

I will explain each of these in more detail in a moment. But first, I would like you to realize that this is the point where you have to develop the discipline to save money because each strategy requires setting aside a portion of your income. You will have to make tough choices about how you spend your money, but just as anyone who has worked hard to acquire and grow wealth has had to apply themselves to these same tasks, so do you. There are no shortcuts at this point, but it's not as painful as you might have previously believed, especially if you have been practicing Steps 1 through 5 and embracing an overall attitude of abundance through the techniques you have already mastered.

Here are the next logical steps, proven strategies that I use for myself and my clients. When you take conscious action to make these changes in your life, I truly believe this advice will help you achieve the financial means to support your lifestyle, financial security, and financial independence.

Establishing Your Own Financial Means

When you receive your paycheck, remember to take a moment and quietly thank yourself for getting up in the mornings and making the effort to show up, doing the best you can, and receiving this sum in return. Send out the energy of gratitude to your employer, to your customers, to your clients, to your partners, and to anyone who contributed to bringing this fortune to you.

Know that every check or deposit to your account is a gift, whether it's your paycheck, a bonus, a reimbursement, a loan, a tax refund, a trust distribution, or an inheritance. Be thankful for it now, for there is no guarantee that another one is coming.

There are millions of ways you could spend your check. However, I want you to put a portion of it aside for an account that you deem "My Divine Purpose Account." This is money for you to support your dream, separate from a general-purpose account, which is used for all your day-to-day bills.

This is your first critical step in ultimately establishing the financial means to fund your deepest desires, those that align with your core values. Whether it's to take time off to volunteer in Africa, to start your own business, to purchase a home, or to go to school, honor your most important dream and invest in it today. In other words: *Pay yourself first.*

If you feel you simply can't set something aside, I am challenging you to still do so; otherwise, you may well join the millions of people who are deeply in debt in this world and stuck in scarcity for what seems like forever. Cash flow is the lifeblood of any business, and this holds true for you as an individual; cash flow is your key to your financial success.

And whatever you do: *Pay yourself first.* Did I just say that again? Yes, because it's *that* important.

EXERCISE:
Jump-Start Your Savings

You simply cannot spend more than you earn on a consistent basis. So you have two options: Earn more or spend less. This exercise will help you take a hard look at how much you really need, and see if you can find ways to cut back—otherwise, you will need to increase your income stream.

To jump-start your savings, the quicker fix at this point is to *spend less*. Let's start with that. First, review your monthly bank and credit-card statements. As you look at these, say "Thank you" for all the wonderful experiences you have had and the useful and beautiful purchases you made. Now comes the challenging part: You have to assess if you truly needed to make those purchases; you need to get a handle on your spending and the true cost of living.

Next time, you might consciously choose not to spend extra money on a new phone or new pair of shoes when you don't really need them, but this doesn't mean you deprive yourself. On the contrary, it's about paving the way for you to truly get what you want. You may not be able to prance around in your "savings" today like you would strut around in your new shoes, but when you're committed to going after your own dreams, you won't feel the need to impress other people (and feed your ego) anymore. Instead, you'll be content knowing you take actions in line with your deepest desires.

Here are some of the best techniques for starting to cut your spending and daily expenses, thus freeing up the money you don't think you have for savings. Challenge yourself to see how many you can do, and each time you bring an expense down, save that money for your dreams and your future. Ready? Set? Go!

- Highlight any recurring expenses on your statements or bills that you could potentially cut, such as newspaper, magazine, or online subscriptions.

- Could you cut back on your cable or your cell-phone bill?

- How many times have you eaten out? Do you think you could reduce the frequency? Be honest about what you truly need versus what you simply want.

- Are a lot of your transactions at retail outlets, and you can't remember what you bought that cost $82.55? Which of those are debits? Make a point to keep every single retail sales slip, even the ones for coffee or a book, and match them up with your online statement once a week. This will raise awareness of where your money is truly going. Track all your cash purchases, too, and what you spend ordering things online. You'll be surprised by what you can do without buying when you become conscious of what you are actually spending.

- Can you lower your daily travel costs by taking public transport more often or by biking to work? Can you carpool with neighbors?

- Can you bring down your monthly housing costs by downsizing now that the kids are gone or by moving to a lower-rent area?

- Can you renegotiate your insurance rates?

- Can you get a better deal on interest rates you pay on existing debt?

Some of these are not easy options, and I know there is always a cost to living. It might sound so basic, but I bring this to your attention because you may hate having to scrutinize what you're spending. You have a choice about your living costs. You can choose where you live, what type of home you live in, and what kind of car you drive. You can choose to go out or eat at home. You can control these costs. The less you spend on things you don't really need or desire, the more you have to save and invest, in order to design the life that fulfills your vision of abundance.

Establishing Your Own Financial Security

Next, let's focus on your financial security and why it's so important. People often cast aside goals to fund emergencies—they might have unexpected auto repairs or lose their job. Urgent and unanticipated issues always come up, but they don't have to ruin you financially. When you cut back on current spending, use some of that money to build a separate Emergency Fund instead of dipping into your Divine Purpose Account.

Set aside enough cash in your Emergency Fund to cover at least three to six months of expenses; we call this "liquid cash." *Liquid* means access to cash immediately at your disposal without any penalties and fees. A few ways to do this is to automatically contribute to a savings account in cash or make conservative investments you can access without penalty if an emergency arises.

Nowadays, many financial institutions will also lend against your investment portfolios, and given low interest rates, you could keep your money invested and borrow against your investments in order to fund an emergency. Check with your bank or financial advisor to see if this is possible. Of course, this option works only if you have substantial investments already and are committed to paying back these amounts borrowed in good time, so the money owed doesn't become long-term ongoing debt.

Insurance is another way to mitigate your risk of disaster. Talk to your agent and have him or her review your home and auto coverage. You also want to look into health insurance and might want to consider life and disability insurance depending on your situation. Insurance premiums add to your expenses, but when a major emergency happens, you'll be truly thankful you have the coverage. It gives you peace of mind simply knowing that you are protected from potential disasters.

Establishing Your Own Financial Independence

This next section is golden! Please pay attention because it will change your life. It's about how to secure your financial *independence*, and I refer to it as growing your Money Tree.

What is a Money Tree? I'm not talking about a bonsai or jade plant that purports to bring good luck and prosperity. I'm talking about building an investment portfolio that keeps growing and that will ultimately generate enough passive income to cover your chosen lifestyle.

Just imagine what you would do if you knew you didn't have to work. You could quit your job and spend more time with your family, or you could travel more. You could take on a job you've always wanted but didn't pursue because the pay was too low. Or maybe you would stay in your current job, but you would get rid of annoying clients and choose to work only with people you like.

Whatever financial freedom looks like to you, it won't happen unless you take conscious action to plant a Money Tree. Remember the phrase "The grass is greener where you water it"? Well, I'm going to help you grow not just grass, but a big, fat tree that will generate enough income to cover the lifestyle you want.

EXERCISE:
Grow Your Money Tree

Here are the basic steps in this process:

1. Calculate How Much of a "Nut" You Need. First, figure out how much money you need every year to live comfortably. Creating a traditional budget is one technique that will help you. This was covered in Step 5, so be sure you have completed it. Your budget informs how much you need to live on each month to maintain your current lifestyle. In Money Tree terms, we call this your "nut."

Alternatively, you could look at your monthly take-home pay after taxes. Do you have money left over after paying your bills? If yes, how much do you save every month? If you don't save, how much of a deficit do you have each month? This equation will also get you to your monthly "nut":

Take-Home Pay – Savings + Deficit = Monthly Nut

Multiply your monthly "nut" by 12, and you have your annual lifestyle number. It's now time to determine how big a tree you will need to generate this income for you.

2. Determine the Size of Your Tree. Most people know they need to save, but they don't know how much. That number depends largely on your lifestyle. Someone with a modest lifestyle needs a smaller Money Tree. A more extravagant lifestyle means a bigger tree is needed to sustain it.

I've created the following table that lists different lifestyle figures on the far left. Find the one that is closest to your annual lifestyle number.

The right column lists the size of investment portfolio that could cover your annual lifestyle. The prudent withdrawal rate in the financial industry is 4 percent, which means that a well-balanced investment portfolio can sustain an annual payout of 4 percent of its value without risking much of the principal. In other words, if you have a million-dollar portfolio, you can receive a stream of income of $40,000 a year for the rest of your life and may still have a million dollars or more left. If you don't want to leave any money behind for loved ones or a charity, you can bump up your withdrawal rate to 5 percent and won't need as big a Money Tree. I share this for you to get an idea of how big a Money Tree is required to cover your expenses.

Money Tree Calculation		
Annual Lifestyle	**Size of Money Tree**	
	4% withdrawal	5% withdrawal
$ 20,000	$ 500,000	$400,000
$ 30,000	$ 750,000	$ 600,000
$ 40,000	$ 1,000,000	$ 800,000
$ 50,000	$ 1,250,000	$ 1,000,000
$ 60,000	$ 1,500,000	$ 1,200,000
$ 70,000	$ 1,750,000	$ 1,400,000
$ 80,000	$ 2,000,000	$ 1,600,000
$ 90,000	$ 2,250,000	$ 1,800,000
$ 100,000	$ 2,500,000	$ 2,000,000
$ 150,000	$ 3,750,000	$ 3,000,000
$ 200,000	$ 5,000,000	$ 4,000,000
$ 250,000	$ 6,250,000	$ 5,000,000

3. Water Your Tree—Consistent Investing. Now that you understand the size tree you need, don't faint! I know these numbers may look larger than some lottery jackpots, but I encourage you to expand your imagination and allow yourself to believe that you could indeed accumulate this much. I'll show you how.

There are three critical factors that directly impact your tree's growth: time, market performance, and regular contributions. The more years that you have to save and invest, the more each dollar can work for you through the power of compounding. If time is not on your side, then it falls on you to sock away as much as you can with each paycheck. Most people rely heavily on the rate of return and take on more risk than they can truly tolerate in hopes of making a bigger return on their investment. Everyone can handle making more money, but you need a strong stomach (and lots of sleeping aids) to handle market volatility and down markets.

Instead, I suggest getting started now and contributing as much and as frequently as you can to a well-balanced investment portfolio. I've included a table that shows the monthly investment required to grow your Money Tree, assuming an 8 percent rate of return:

Power of Compounding (8% rate of return)			
Monthly Investment	20 years	30 years	40 years
$ 100	$ 59,767	$ 151,123	$ 353,855
$ 150	$ 89,681	$ 226,685	$ 530,783
$ 200	$ 119,575	$ 302,246	$ 707,711
$ 300	$ 179,632	$ 453,370	$ 1,061,566
$ 400	$ 239,149	$ 604,492	$ 1,415,422
$ 500	$ 298,337	$ 755,615	$ 1,769,277
$ 700	$ 418,512	$ 1,057,862	$ 2,476,988
$ 1,000	$ 597,874	$ 1,511,231	$ 3,538,554
$ 2,000	$ 1,195,748	$ 3,022,461	$ 7,077,109

Let's go through an example. Let's say that your annual lifestyle figure is $50,000. From the Money Tree calculation table, you found that you need a $1,000,000 tree to cover your living expenses.

The next question is: How much do you need to sock away every month to build a $1,000,000 portfolio? It depends on how long a time horizon you have. If your time horizon is 20 years, you need to contribute $2,000 a month. If you are looking at 30 years, then your monthly contribution goes down to $700. The amount is smaller because you have more time to let your tree grow. But if you can wait 40 years before drawing down on this portfolio, then you only need to sock away $300 a month!

These numbers are just guidelines. There are many planning tools online that can help you determine this and run different scenarios that factor in inflation, taxes, and varying investment returns.

In short, there are two main levers you can pull to grow your tree: time and contributions. The more you save and invest, the less time it takes for you to reach your goal. I suggest opening a brokerage or retirement account and automating transfers on a monthly basis so you don't have to think about it.

Talk to a financial professional who can help you assess your situation, goals, risk tolerance, and time horizon and help you develop a road map and investment strategy. (For more on this, please see Appendix: Adding a Financial Advisor to Your A-Team.)

Again, you can play with compounding calculators and change the growth rate, but I generally don't recommend this. You need to take some risk to try to earn 8 percent, but if you're a relatively new investor, I don't want you to amp up your risk beyond your level of comfort to try to grow your Money Tree faster. It's more important to just get started.

Plant your Money Tree today!

Before leaving this topic, let me just add a few more important points about investing and risk. Investing your money involves a willingness to take some risk. In fact, there is risk in everything you do, even when you do nothing. When you leave your money in cash form, you risk losing purchasing power due to inflation. The cost of living goes up every year, as is evident in the rising prices of gas, food, stamps, education, and so on. By not investing, you risk outliving your savings.

Likewise, when you think you're playing it safe in life, you are still vulnerable. By not investing in your divine purpose, you risk depleting your life energy in trying to make others and your ego happy, which can leave you spiritually and emotionally broken in the end.

Also understand that every investment has an opportunity cost. What that means is when I invest $1,000 in Apple stock, then I'm choosing to forgo other investment opportunities that I could have made with that money. Similarly, when you spend your weekends working, you may be forgoing the opportunity to hang out with your friends or family. You are constantly making trade-offs with your money, time, and energy. It all comes down to this: What are the trade-offs that you are willing to make?

Why Is Wilma Still Waiting?

When it comes to investing, many people who reach out to me for advice say they wish they had started saving and investing decades ago. They realize now that if they had begun earlier, they would have had many more years to compound their financial wealth. How nice it would be if they could turn back the hands of time. This holds true with compounding your spiritual wealth. I know at least one woman who wishes she could have a second chance in life, a creative woman I like to call "Waiting Wilma."

Wilma has dreamed of showcasing her paintings since she graduated 30 years ago with a master of fine arts from a prestigious art school. Her vision of exhibiting her art continues to occupy her mind—she still talks about it today—but she can't find the time to actually paint. She says this is because her daughter's family lives down the street and relies on her help. Wilma thought she'd be free to paint once her grandchild was off to school, but then along came another grandchild, and then another, and then a fourth.

When all four grandchildren became relatively independent, Wilma's father had a stroke, and her mother needed help getting him to multiple doctor appointments. To relieve her stress, Wilma plays golf regularly and goes on vacation with her friends and family. She also teaches painting classes to supplement her social-security income.

Now at 74, Wilma admits she has enjoyed her life and the times she connected with her family and friends. But she carries a deep sense of frustration for not having made any time for her own art over the last three decades. She never devoted herself to fulfilling her dream. Worse yet, she knows what actions she should have taken, but didn't—a fact that serves to add salt to the wounds. If she had only started ten years ago to simply paint one painting a month, or started talking to gallery owners, or developed relationships with other artists, she'd be so much further along. Instead, she's in the same place she was when she first finished art school.

On the other hand, she does feel wiser, and this wisdom may eventually come through in her painting. She met quite a few people from the art world over the years, and some of them might still remember her; maybe they could open some doors? Perhaps it's not too late. But if Wilma really wants to realize her lifelong dream, she must stop procrastinating; she needs to minimize distractions, and she needs to start taking conscious steps to paint *today*.

EXERCISE:
The Devil Is in the Distractions

I would love it if I could simply wave a magic wand and get rid of all the pesky distractions that keep me from being productive and moving ahead with my goals at work and at home. If you find distractions keep you from your greatest good, here are some practical tips:

- **What's Bugging You?** Start by evaluating the kinds of distractions that vie for your attention on any given day. Find ways to minimize the worst ones or get rid of them entirely. What actions do you need to take? Do you need help from someone else? Get the help you need to rid your work space, your home office, and your house of any unnecessary distractions.

- **Turn Off All Your Social-Media Sites.** Constantly watching for updates on all your social-media feeds eats up far more time than you probably think. You don't really have to answer the phone every time it rings or constantly check to see who has tweeted, texted, and e-mailed, but you might have picked up this habit. If you really need to check messages regularly when you have important goals to accomplish, set a timer for 55 minutes and when it goes off, you can take five minutes to see at a glance what is new and reply to anything urgent. When your five minutes are up, log out of the social-media sites, and set the timer again for 55 minutes. You will be amazed how you can get used to just checking your favorite sites on the hour.

- **Carve Out Priority Time to Get Your Priority Action Items Completed.** If certain tasks deserve or require your undivided focus, turn off all your devices and just pay attention to the most important action item until it's done. Be kind to yourself and simply ask "How important is this?" Remember, when you value your true worth, you can figure out more accurately what your top priorities are, and you can move forward in a much more powerful, more effective, more self-loving, and less distracted manner.

- **Allow Yourself Occasional Distractions.** We all want to have fun and give ourselves a break once in a while. Listen to your body's signals. When you feel tapped out, allow yourself time to reboot: Go for a walk, watch TV, or engage in activities that bring you pleasure. Just be mindful of how much time and how many resources you expend while on a break, set a time to return to your important tasks, and hold yourself to it.

EXERCISE:
Creating a Conscious Activity Plan

Now it's time to take action. The goal of this exercise is to plan how to better allocate your time, money, and energy in order to create the life you want—a life that contains both spiritual and financial wealth in the right balance for you.

When you truly value something, you must set aside the resources and make it a priority. For instance, I wish I could squeeze in more yoga, which reflects my core values of both health and spiritual connection. I can *say* these are my core values all day long, but unless I actually budget my time and money for classes, the yoga won't happen. By committing two hours every Thursday afternoon in my calendar and paying for a series, I increase the chances that yoga will become a more regular part of my routine. Now it's your turn.

- Think of the activities you keep telling yourself you want to do. Notice that these activities should naturally align with one of your core values. Whether it's taking classes, volunteering, or being outdoors more often, list everything you can think of. Rank them all in order, starting with the one that is most important to you at this stage. We all hold many values, but certain values become greater priorities at different times in our lives. Again, ignore the "shoulds" and just stay attuned with what is meaningful to *you*.

- Write down each Core-Value Activity in the chart below and list an action you could take to make this activity a reality, plus a date to get started. Examples include: signing up for classes, researching new jobs, or reaching out to your friends.

- Find a regular time and budget specific dollars to the activities that are most important. You may need to reallocate time and money from other activities that are not as high a priority. For instance, maybe you are paying a gym membership that you would be willing to let go of and instead spend more time hiking outdoors.

- This worksheet will help you focus your resources on what's important to you so you can manifest the life you want. It forms a plan of action that you can look at each week to keep you on track.

Since life changes, come back to this exercise on a regular basis and be prepared to continue to adjust your activities to favor those where the expenditure of time and money are worth the most to you.

Conscious Activity Plan			
Core-Value Activity (ranked by priority)	Action Required in Order to Get Started, and Date to Begin	Amount of Time You Will Commit	Amount of Money You Will Commit

Let Your Divine Decide

You now know you make choices every minute. Sometimes you decide with your stomach, sometimes with your mind, and sometimes with your heart. My recommendation is this: *Let your divine decide!* Take a deep breath, center yourself in your body, feel your presence here and now, and step into your Divine Self. Then listen. What does your Divine Self tell you to do?

If you can't hear that voice, try to feel it. When you think about doing something or buying something, does it bring you deep joy? Do you open up and feel more connected to who you are? Or, do you feel your old ego at work, creating tightness in your body and bringing up familiar feelings of attachment, guilt, shame, or inferiority?

Try this instead. Imagine you have everything you need (which, by the way, you do). Feeling this sense of abundance and fulfillment at your core, do you still want this item or job or whatever? Thanking God or the universe for all you already have, what choice do you want to make?

145

When you feel you are living in abundance, you do have it all. You have the freedom to make the right choices and spend your time and energy on things aligned with your core values. Plus you don't have to accomplish all your goals completely on your own. The next step describes how you can connect with other like-minded people and collaborate with them to make your dreams come true.

When your actions and values align, so many wonderful things happen. You are no longer afraid to speak up because you know your words matter. You act with courage because your self-worth is supported. You feel love for yourself and know you are loved. You know you have power, and you choose to wield it with loving-kindness. You don't need to shame others or make anyone feel bad to make yourself feel better. You stop idolizing and envying others. You know you are enough, and you have enough.

Scarcity or abundance? The choice is yours. *Which do you choose?*

Key Messages about Committing to Conscious Action

- Whether you are aware of it or not, you always have the power of choice.

- Your life is the sum total of all the choices you make.

- Regardless of where you are in life, now is the best time to get started in achieving your goals.

- Time and regular investments are two powerful ingredients for wealth. Get started now regardless of the size of investment.

- Saying no to distractions is saying yes to your Divine Self.

STEP 7

Connect and Collaborate

Every human being is a divine soul, blessed with unique gifts. Just imagine what the world would be like if every person manifested his or her highest potential. I would love to live in a world like that. By creating abundance in your life, you contribute abundance to the world, collaborating with every other soul. Hence, the more each of us aligns with our Divine Self, the more we can collectively elevate the level of consciousness in the world.

I truly believe we're meant to help each other so we can all live abundantly. There's more than enough to go around. Just because you have happiness and security doesn't mean there's any less for me or anyone else. We can all be happy and secure. I'd rather be surrounded by people who are grateful for what they have, even if it's not a lot, and realize there's enough to share. I know from experience that sharing actually makes me feel even richer because I can see how my acts of kindness make a positive impact. It feels good to give and to share, and this creates even more gratitude all around, perpetuating a collective loop of abundance for us all. Step 7 focuses on how you can use the principles of connection and collaboration to help you fulfill your dreams and work with others to build a better world.

And guess what? This is a really fun part of the whole process because as you reach out, you will find that sharing increases happiness, too, not just for the person who receives your kindness, but also for you. A 2008 study by Harvard Business School professor Michael Norton and his colleagues showed that spending your income on other people gives more of a boost to your happiness than spending that same money on yourself.

The Joy of Giving

You don't have to have millions to make a meaningful gift. My grandmother loves to give. She spends her days making food to share with members of her church. I remember going with her to forage for foods such as nettles, seaweed, and acorns so she could make delicious Korean treats for her community members. She eats from her garden, walks to church, and lives quite comfortably according to her humble standards.

My grandmother has a special savings plan for her social-security checks: Every five years, she gives each of her 20 grandchildren and great-grandchildren a thousand dollars. She doesn't have a sizable bank account, and chooses to live below her means. She truly believes she has more than enough, and because of that she feels rich when her checks come in the mail. She carefully calculates her resources and allocates them according to her core values: religious faith and family. It brings her so much joy to express her love by saving every dollar and presenting a gift to each family member and donating money to her church.

Billions of people all over the world live modest lives and still feel they have enough to share with others. Regardless of the amount, we all have gifts we can bestow. We each have a purpose and something special and unique to offer. It is a noble quest for us to search for what we'd like to give or share, and to align ourselves with that gift. By doing so, we will feel that abundance lies within and around us every day.

The Spirit of Giving Keeps on Giving

On this topic, I'm reminded of a woman named Jane whose son died at the age of 13 after losing a long battle against cancer. Family and friends came to her side as she mourned his death. Her burning desire to give back to the world helped her get through some of her darkest moments. She recognized how blessed she had been by the time she did have with her son and the supportive community that came together for her, and how much she had to share with the world.

As she stood by her son's grave site, she initially thought about how much her son loved reading and how he always carried a book around. She felt a strong urge to give back and envisioned teaching reading in low-income and other deprived communities. Soon after, she started visiting prisons and began reading with the prisoners on a regular basis. Jane felt so full of joy that she started a bookmobile service to deliver books to children in poorer neighborhoods where they didn't have access to a public library.

Jane's heart continued to grow. For her next project, she set up a soup kitchen to serve the less fortunate. She made sure the dining room had tables and chairs where guests could sit and be served with dignity, rather than having them wait in a long line. Jane recruited her friends and neighbors to help with serving, and everyone enjoyed the warm and respectful community atmosphere.

These acts of service pulled Jane out of her overwhelming sadness over losing her son. She knew deep down that she had a divine purpose, and she committed herself to sharing her knowledge, her skills, her resources, and herself with others. Jane clearly decided not to waste her unique gifts and talents, and as a result she felt immense gratitude for her blessings and a sincere desire to share.

But it didn't stop there. Jane continued to connect with others and collaborate with them to find out how she could make an even greater impact and reach more people in need. She continued

149

to engage her friends to help make each of her visions a reality. By working together, they deepened their relationships with each other and collectively produced a better life for everyone they reached out to.

While perhaps it's easier just to write a check or merely support friends and causes online, I feel no substitute exists for getting out and personally connecting with other people and the natural world. Such interactions keep us feeling vital and happy. Laughing and smiling together in a social setting is a basic human joy. If you spend most of your time alone or living a solitary life, you miss out on a deeply fulfilling aspect of human existence. Connecting with others is part of our divine abundance.

EXERCISE:
Four Strategies to Feel Connected

Jane's natural drive to be connected to others in a meaningful way is a common human trait throughout the world. We are social beings, and it's in our nature to connect with other people in our daily lives. We all share this universe together, and what one does affects another. How can you start sharing your abundance today? This exercise gives you some practical ways to connect with the outside world and to celebrate and enjoy our abundant planet.

1. **Connect with Nature.** When you are outside, notice how all living things are free to be what they are, and each creature is a divine part of the universe. We are all connected within the same ecosystem and have our rightful place in the big scheme of things. Nature has no ego to worry about. Does a bird worry it's not a tree? Or a tree fret that it's not as grand as a mountain or as refreshing as a stream? Each day, appreciate how your actions can contribute to reaching a critical mass in consciousness. Imagine the collective impact we could

make if we all did our part to conserve water, energy, and clean air or even made small shifts in our lifestyles to support our planet, such as switching to organic, pesticide-free produce.

2. **Connect with an Organization.** Whether you connect with a corporation, a public entity, a religious or charitable organization, or any community of people, acknowledge how your involvement makes a difference. Millions of people are waiting for you to show up, depending on you to make the choice to help them. You have the power to affect a community on the other side of the world, or right in your own backyard.

   Think of how many people that organization reaches within its employee base and externally with its vendors, partners, and customers. With each purchase you make, every day of honest work, or each hour you volunteer, you impact an organized global system that is infinitely greater than you. Your actions have a ripple effect throughout the world. By showing up 100 percent, you can influence an organization and its constituents.

3. **Connect with Another Person.** Brighten someone's day with a smile. Communicate to someone that you are thinking about him or her. Lighten someone else's load and help out in any way you can. You have skills someone else could benefit from, so try sharing your time, talents, and knowledge. Become a mentor in your field of expertise or based on your life experience. On the flip side, try reaching out to someone who can give you the support you need. (I will dive deeper into how to connect with others to build your personal Abundance Loop team later in this chapter.)

4. **Connect with Your Divine Self.** Spend time with yourself in quiet contemplation. Refer back to the meditation and breath exercises in Step 2 to help you with this. Listen carefully to your own divine wisdom because it guides you to achieve your potential and enjoy your greatest good. Use affirmations to remind you of your true worth—positive statements to reinforce the belief that you already have abundance in your life. I have included some sample affirmations about abundance at the end of Step 8 to reinforce the important concepts that make up the Abundance Loop.

    If you have a hard time sitting still, you can connect with your divine by engaging in an activity where you get so engrossed that you lose yourself. Whether it's writing, painting, cooking, playing the piano, running, biking, or skiing, find the time to do something that you absolutely love and feel totally connected with, so much so that the world just melts away. The key is to let everything else go, be totally present in the moment, and experience the joy of being one with yourself, with your divine, and with everything around you.

Set High Boundaries and Respect Where Others Are

Ultimately, this book offers ways to help you transform your life through awareness and abundance. If you are ready to embrace these concepts and begin enacting them, excellent; but be aware that not everyone in your family or in your circle of friends may be thrilled to hear all about your new philosophy. As you start to change your behavior, you may experience a shift in your close relationships.

Think about it this way: Imagine you have been away for a long time and come back home to revisit old friends. Notice how you end up talking about the same things as back in the "good old days." When you try to change the conversation to include new ways of thinking, or you exhibit a change of personality (perhaps you now come across as more confident or self-assured), how would you imagine they respond?

You wouldn't be the only person to experience this kind of resistance. As you mature and align with your divine purpose, friends who have grown accustomed to your being a particular way may feel uncomfortable with your transformation. Losing these friends because you have grown and changed can bring up emotions of sadness, anger, and grief from you or from them. Just be aware of that.

It's important to talk to your friends about your desire to grow into your best self. If they aren't supportive in both words and actions, you may have outgrown the relationship. This has happened to me. I had to let a few friendships dissolve, and although I love these individuals, I knew if I continued to tolerate their negativity and kept dimming my own light, I would be doing a disservice to myself and to them. I knew I needed to set firmer boundaries so I would not be dragged down with them, back into a scarcity mind-set.

I can't expect everyone to think the way I do. I have to respect where people are right now on their own journeys. This is particularly hard when you see someone suffering and you desperately want to help. However, you can only do so much. Ultimately, people must make their own choices and follow their own path. You can give guidance, you can pray for them, but you cannot enable them to stay stuck in unhealthy patterns. Furthermore, you cannot manifest abundance when you're not able to be at your best, which means surrounding yourself with those who want to see you shine.

Friends for Life

By letting go of those who simply couldn't support me, I made room for new, more conscious and abundant people to come into my life. I am so thankful life unfolded the way it did because now we talk about our dreams and how we make them come true. We attend retreats on topics we each enjoy; we read similar books and discuss them together. We connect more deeply because we feel comfortable being and expressing our authentic selves with each other, without pretenses or artificial barriers between us. Later in the book, I offer techniques you can use to network and to find new, like-minded friends. I encourage you to apply these in your life.

Friendships can be like banks accounts. When you earn money, you make a deposit into your savings account, and when you need money, you make a withdrawal. The more you save, the more you have to tide you over during lean times. Similarly, when you treat someone well, you add to the friendship (making a deposit in your "trust bank"), and when you hurt someone, you deplete trust. If a friend keeps withdrawing from your friendship account, she will deplete you over time. She may not be aware that she is doing that, so you may want to communicate how you feel about how her behaviors are affecting you.

Check in with yourself regularly to make sure you have reserves left in the account and it doesn't get overdrawn. Depending on how long you've been friends, or the intensity of your relationship, you may have built up a significant mutual "trust account."

Communicate Your Dream

Talking with other like-minded people about what you want for your life often hastens progress toward your dreams. It has happened for me many times over the past several years, after I embarked on my new path and while writing this book. But this is not what happened to a man in his late 30s named Will. No new supporters came to help him. Let's see if you can guess why.

Will worked as a café manager when I first met him, and, of course, I asked my favorite question: "What does abundance mean to you?"

He seemed rather taken aback because no one had asked him that before, and he said, "I know most people would say money, but it's not the money itself. Money is just a tool for getting what I want."

I asked him what he really wanted, and he said he'd like to have his own business. He wanted to open a bar, the kind of place where people would come after a long day of work to chill before going home to their families. I asked him, "So are you socking away money from this job to open your bar?"

His answer stopped me in my tracks because he was so blunt: "No, no. By the time this job pays me enough money to start my own business, I'll be dead."

Will had a clear vision about his bar, but he didn't have the funds to start it, nor was he able to save money. When I asked him if he'd talked to anyone about his dream, he said no. When I prodded him a little further, he admitted he hadn't said anything out loud because he was afraid of failing. He'd be embarrassed if his business didn't take off and feared he would never hear the end of it from his friends and family—clearly, Will found himself stuck deep in a Scarcity Loop.

As you know, when you let fear drive your choices, you end up with scarce results. Will's fear of failure kept him from reaching out to others for help. By not communicating his desires to anyone, he couldn't move forward to manifest them into reality.

But let's look at a similar situation. In this case, Carl worked as a bartender and regularly talked to his patrons about how much he loves brewing beer. One day, his regular customer Jay heard Carl talking about his dream of opening his own brewpub and piped up that he had a buddy who wanted to invest in a brewery. Jay brought his friend Michael to the bar, and the two hit it off.

Michael had retired from the corporate world and wanted to own a pub, where he could hang out in the afternoons; but he didn't know how to actually brew beer. The two men discussed their own strengths and values and hashed out a plan. They are now business partners and successfully run a bar together serving delicious craft beer (and excellent pub food, I might add).

Let's look at Carl's Abundance Loop:

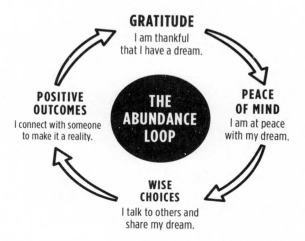

If you really want your dream to come true, start taking action and start connecting. Build a team of like-minded people to help support you in your quest to accomplish it. The next section deals with this concept and offers specific techniques to help you grow your circle of supporters.

Who's on Your Team?

In *Good to Great*, Jim Collins talks about how great companies get the right people on the bus, the wrong people off the bus, and the right people in the right seats. This holds for life, too: You are the driver of your own life. Who do you want on your bus?

When building your A-Team—your Abundance Team—let your divine decide. As with the other decisions in your life, go back to your values and clearest intentions. You know best what matters to you. Refer to those core values and your inner wisdom to help you navigate the relationships and interactions you need in your life.

Use discernment, and carefully choose the people you can trust, supporters who have the capacity, the competency, the willingness, and the loving spirit to come through for you and for your vision. I'm not saying you have to completely reshape your current circle of friends, but when you focus on manifesting your divine wealth, you must identify those who can enhance your growth and help keep you moving forward in the Abundance Loop. Personal growth is a challenging enough process, and the more you feel supported along the way, the more fun and success you will have.

EXERCISE:
Choosing the Members of Your A-Team

Here are some questions to help you determine if someone belongs on your A-Team. Feel free to come up with your own criteria as well. But in general, when you approach someone for help, think about the following points:

- Does this person have an attitude of gratitude?

- Do I trust this person to really support my dream?

- Can I count on this person to be there for me when I need him or her?

- What do I respect about this person?

- Has this person given me sound advice in the past?

- Has this person stepped up for me in the past?

- Does this person have a collaborative spirit, or is it all about him or her?

- What core competencies does this person have?

- Does this person live in alignment with his or her own core values?

- Does this person respect my values?

Ultimately, you want to know that each person can step up and be there for you and not get in the way of your transformation. You want someone you can call on when the going gets tough, to help keep you accountable for the goals you set for yourself, or to call you on your "stuff" in a loving manner when you display ego-driven behaviors that are out of sync with your values and highest intentions.

It's hard to see your own blind spots. You need other people in order to grow and keep you on the Abundance Loop journey. And you must be committed to do all these same things for others when they call on you. We are all in this together.

Here is an example of a chart you might construct to take an inventory of who is in your life and how they support you in various ways. It shows you who is, and who is not, on your side and also reveals any gaps that let you know it's time to get out and meet someone new to help you. To do this, you might try some of the networking techniques mentioned in the upcoming pages. Please remember that there is no shame in seeking help. No one achieves success alone.

My Abundance Loop Team			
What do I want?	Who also wants this for me?	Who doesn't want this for me?	Who can support me?
Find a new job.	My best friend who believes in personal growth.	Co-workers who tell me this is how life is.	Career counselor. Life coach.
Grow a Money Tree so I can quit my job.	My best friend who encourages me to save more.	My friend Marie, who gets jealous and upset when I have nice things.	Financial advisor.*
Lose weight.	My partner.	My restaurant buddy.	Personal trainer.
Be an artist.	My artist friends.	Co-workers; family.	Creative community.
Donate to my favorite charity.	The charity recipients. Other donors to the charity.	My husband.	My tax or financial advisor.* Development director.

Please note that the questions for finding a financial advisor are a little different. I have included a list of those in the Appendix to help you make that important decision.

Voices Being Heard

Tara had a vision to start an online magazine to encourage women to "wear" their voice. She was passionate about helping women to look and feel their best by being themselves and dressing in ways that truly express who they are. As she wrote her blog and talked about her vision, other women stepped forward and contributed their writing, photography, and other creative efforts. She attended at least two networking events a week, organized fashion shows to highlight local artists and designers, and volunteered at a nonprofit that serves low-income women by helping them to feel good about themselves in the workplace through their clothes and attitude.

Everywhere she went, Tara talked about her publication, and new readers subscribed to it every month. After just one year, her project was voted one of the best new magazines in her area.

Tara knew it would take a team of dedicated people to make the magazine fly, and she continued to reach out every day to meet more supporters of her vision. She took deliberate action by getting started with her writing, by collaborating with others, and by sharing her gift. Ultimately, Tara's efforts not only enriched her community, but also enriched her soul.

Connect for Win-Win-Win

Most people's dreams—whether it's changing careers, balancing personal fulfillment with commitments to family, or achieving financial freedom—require the guidance of those who have accomplished what they're aiming for or have resources they can draw upon for support.

If you want to meet business and community people who can help you with your dreams, have you tried *authentic networking*? It's a perfect approach because it starts with a different mind-set than traditional networking, which is getting out to social events and business meetings in the hopes of meeting a client or someone to buy your product or support your cause. When you connect with others to "get" something, you are operating from a place of lack and stuck in the Scarcity Loop.

Authentic networking, on the other hand, is living in the Abundance Loop. It is based on the premise that if you believe that you have something of value to share with other people, you will show up with an abundance mind-set, which is to say you will feel confident and content that you have more than enough, that you *are* more than enough. As you meet potential business or community supporters, you radiate positive energy and others are drawn to your light and your higher vibration.

You not only have a heart to share your special talents, but you also have the wisdom and discernment to detect when someone might deplete your energy. You steer clear. But you also know when you "click" with someone, someone who is ready to step up to help you with your product, service, cause, or whatever you need.

Authentic networkers know it's important to be conscious of the energy and financial flow within their relationships, in order to attract people who, like themselves, are committed to whatever they agree to do. Once you learn to use discernment, you will begin to attract more authentic people in your circle, rather than those who tend to talk a lot but don't actually get much done.

People who get out there and openly reach out to others are grounded in the belief that they have value to offer. They are curious and willing to learn from others. They are open-minded and want to share their skills; they also assume others have knowledge and skills they can benefit from. They attend networking events to make a match for their next project, product launch, or initiative, and are successful because they know that such deals sow seeds of abundance. They exude confidence and charisma and have a win-win-win attitude where not only can two people benefit from each other, but together, they can add value to the world. With all these attributes combined with their pure intentions, how could they ever lose?

EXERCISE:
How to Network Efficiently

Efficient networking is almost entirely about your attitude and your ability to follow up. Here are some of my go-to points for upping your success while attending social meetings or networking events:

- Always walk into a room or an event with the expectation that you will accomplish what you came to do. Intent is a powerful way to open the doors you want to open.

- Show up for all events well groomed and dressed the way that a professional in your field would dress. This is an occasion when you want to dress for the job you want in the future, not the one you might have just now (unless you have your highest-level dream job already).

- Shake hands firmly with people as you meet them. Smile, look them in the eye, and repeat their name a few times in the ensuing conversation to help you remember.

- Collect their business cards and offer them yours. Even if you don't make an immediate connection, you still might wish to contact that person in the future.

- If you're in a busy room and meeting many people, jot a quick note about each person you speak to, especially if you intend to meet with them again as a follow-up.

- Don't make any networking opportunity all about you. Instead, be interested in the views and products of the other people. Ask them sincere questions and engage them to try to find a way that you can both help each other. Look to create a win-win-win situation.

- Develop a relationship, not a deal. Be genuine and focus on getting to know the other person. Look for common interests and highlight their positive traits.

- If you are not a match for what someone needs right now, be gracious and leave the meeting on a positive note. Be thankful that you met them. You never know when they might need your services after all, or you might need theirs.

- If your radar goes up and you sense a person you've just met doesn't share your mind-set and your degree of professionalism, proceed with caution. Your gut instincts are usually right on, so heed any warnings your body or inner wisdom gives you about the people you meet. Politely excuse yourself if you really feel a bad vibe.

Speak Up and Follow Up

When I tell people I want to speak to audiences, most can immediately think of at least one group I should get in front of. That's fantastic! But then I remember I need to follow up. I immediately ask for their contact information so I can stay in touch. Shortly after the meeting, I send them an e-mail and keep the dialogue going.

It is always best to follow up as soon as you can. Most people have short attention spans and new tasks pop up every day. So put yourself out there. When potential opportunities come up, get in front of them. If they don't pan out, that's fine; at least you tried. You gave it a shot. But when you don't take the initiative to reach out, you let potential opportunities slip by. Abundance surrounds you, and it's up to you to manifest it into reality.

If you need to develop supporters, find specific clients, or seek a better career connection, I advise you to put yourself in the path of as many people as you can. You will eventually meet the right people. And don't forget to be thankful at every step, at every meeting. I am a big fan of thank-you notes. The more you appreciate someone's help or their business, the more abundance comes to you. Positive friendships and client relationships are part of your abundant birthright, so make the most of every connection.

Earn a Living Being of Service

The key to abundance keeps coming back to your core values. When you live in alignment with your core values, you feel content, and that is the essence of abundance, of feeling *enough*.

This is particularly true when it comes to finding a job. Don't think of a job as simply trying to earn money. Remember your true purpose is being of service to the world, to your company, to your family, and to yourself.

If you don't have your dream job yet, think about what you enjoy doing. What are you passionate about? What are your gifts? How can you share them with others? I strongly suggest connecting with a career counselor or life coach and exploring different options for how you can earn money and design your life.

Don't give up on your passion, even if it doesn't pay the bills just yet.

Here's the story of a man who keeps his passion alive even though his job is actually in another field entirely.

Meet 50-year-old Sam. He is passionate about playing his trumpet and believes he's being of service through his music, connecting to audiences and collaborating with different bands who hire him whenever they need a trumpet player. He plays whenever he gets a chance.

Sam works full-time as an account manager in a design studio, which pays the bills and gives him the flexibility to travel the world to perform. Sam feels abundant doing what he loves and working in a job that offers both money and time. He communicated to his employer how important his music to him, and got extra days off when he needed to be on the road.

Because Sam feels so grateful to his employer and his music colleagues, he operates at peak levels at work as well as onstage. His music is truly his gift to the world.

I encourage you to share your light with the world. Consider starting a blog, writing a book, posting your art, or performing. Once you put yourself out there, others will give you feedback, and with that feedback, you can continue to hone your skill and clarify your message, your style, your gift.

EXERCISE:
Tips on Being of Service

You don't need to have money to be of service and make an impact. You can leverage your creativity, your time, your energy, your network, or your talents to help make the world more abundant for others and, by doing so, for yourself. The more you give of yourself, the more you get back. By giving back, you declare to the world that you are abundant, that you have more than enough to share with others.

Here are just a few ways that you can be of service to others:

- Be kind and respectful to those around you. Charity begins at home.

- Volunteer to help your friend move or find a job.

- Volunteer at your local food bank or soup kitchen.

- Participate in bike-a-thons, 5Ks, marathons, or triathlons that raise money for causes you admire.

- Donate clothing, furniture, equipment, and other possessions to those in need.

- Sign up for volunteer events with your family and friends.

- Seriously, just Google "volunteer opportunities" and the name of your town or city, and start reaching out. There is no shortage of places that would welcome your help!

(I want to add a quick word of caution here. It's important to understand that when you volunteer, you need to be conscious of how much time and energy you share with others. Many people burn out easily from volunteering, organizing events, leading committees, and raising money. When you start to feel depleted, be sure to take a break. You don't do anyone any favors by running on empty. This holds true financially, emotionally, and physically. You need to maintain your reserves in order to be of service to anyone, including to yourself.)

In the next and final chapter, you will see how all the exercises you've done and all your experiences have now prepared you to step into your light. You will learn to leave behind those dark nights trapped in the Scarcity Loop and celebrate who you are in the Abundance Loop.

Key Messages about Connecting and Collaborating

- Build an Abundance Loop Team with people you trust, who can support your growth.

- Communicate your dreams to others and be open to opportunities.

- There's more than enough to go around, so joyfully collaborate with others.

- Connect with an organization to multiply your impact on the world.

- True wealth, as measured by happiness, lies in being of service.

STEP 8

Celebrate the Freedom to Be You

We're at the final step in this process, the one where you celebrate the freedom to be you! In Step 8, the focus is on integrating, and inspiring you to truly embrace your divine wealth. This information and the last two exercises herein are powerful ways to wrap up and reinforce the Abundance Loop process.

From this point on, you will be living all this material, breathing it, and using it daily to secure freedom from your ego. If you want to find a specific exercise to do again as a refresher, you'll find an index of all 30 exercises at the end of the book. Keep this book handy as you may need it again, especially if scarcity should start to sneak into your abundant world for any reason. You know what to do. Kick it to the curb.

There is one more thing that many, many people wish they were completely free of, and that is *debt*. In a few moments, we're going to get back to our celebration, but first let me offer a note of caution and a short explanation of debt, which is such a huge concern for so many. You probably cringe when you think about debt, but it's not necessarily the big bad downer that everyone seems to think it is.

Remember, debt is just a tool, like a hammer or a saw. It can be used to help you build a strong financial future *or* tear it down. It's up to you to decide how you want to use it. Here's a quick review of how you can use debt to your advantage.

Taking out a mortgage to purchase a home, for example, makes sense—especially when interest rates are low and the interest can be deducted from your taxes. Although a mortgage is a liability on the balance sheet, it is balanced against your home, an asset that can appreciate in value. Likewise, student loans are an excellent resource to help you build your intellectual capital, which brings you earning power throughout your career.

Borrowing money to start a business is a sound decision when you have a strong business case and are confident in your ability to pay back those loans within the terms you negotiated. In these ways, loans are liabilities right now, but ultimately they can help you build wealth in the long run.

It's Another Dreaded D-Word

Here's where the feeling of dread comes from when you hear the word *debt*. Millions of people in our world suffer from overwhelming debt. This happens when you use credit cards or loans to finance a lifestyle that you cannot really afford. It's so exciting to realize you can buy something new, like a car, a computer, furniture, clothes, or vacations, but when you buy anything on credit and only make minimum payments you're on a slippery slope. At first, paying $30' a month seems affordable, but when you keep charging things up, the minimum payments quickly get out of control, the length of repayment time gets stretched out, and you feel you're constantly treading water. That's when you shut down, feeling petrified to even open your statements.

At this point, fear and anxiety put you in a stranglehold and you can't break free of the pattern, severely stuck in the Scarcity Loop. Next stops could be hopelessness and sleepless nights, collection calls, and insolvency. Before your debt becomes this kind of a disaster, you really need to face up to it and try to resolve it, no matter how scared you are.

The techniques from this book will help you improve your finances, but they are not an immediate fix. If your debt is out of hand, or getting out of hand, I would suggest that you see a financial counselor who can help you understand your options. Or, you may want to see if there's a Debtors Anonymous or Underearners Anonymous meeting in your area. Ultimately you are the one who has to decide what you want your future to look like: shrouded in fear or confidently under control?

Speaking of fear, you can perhaps realize now that fear works similarly to the way debt does. Fear itself is not bad, but when you succumb to it and let it overwhelm you, you can get caught and spiral downward. But when you use each of the steps described in the Abundance Loop process, you become conscious of your fear and willing to do what it takes to get out from under its power. Your fear then becomes a catalyst to help you live your best life.

Next up is a story about Helen, whose fear turned out to be a powerful motivator for her.

Could It Happen to You?

Helen and her husband didn't have easy lives, but they were hardworking people trying to make the best life for themselves and their infant daughter. They got by until a series of losses hit them hard, and they hit rock bottom. It was financially and emotionally devastating when she and her family were evicted because they couldn't pay their rent. The couple and their baby girl faced living on the streets.

Fortunately, they were given access to a government-sponsored shelter, though this meant that the three of them were crammed in a tiny room in a building that sheltered 20 other homeless families. Helen felt that she'd lost her dignity. She hated being told when to be home for "curfew," what to do, and when to eat because the shelter had so many rules. She wore slippers in the showers to avoid fungus, she slept with earplugs to muffle all the noise, and she worried constantly about the safety of her daughter.

Helen was furious about losing her home, but she refused to allow this setback to break her and her family. She and her husband made a conscious choice to work hard together and try to get back on their feet. Her husband went to school to get certified in construction management, and Helen studied cosmetology.

Living in the shelter was both a blessing and a curse. The shelter provided therapy, and Helen found the emotional support she desperately needed to overcome her past and present demons. She realized she couldn't keep waiting for an apology from those who hurt her: her mother who had abused her, her father who had abandoned the family when she was an infant, a family "friend" who had sexually abused her, or her friends who had not offered to take Helen and her family in.

Helen's Rise from Homelessness

Helen realized that she could go on thinking of herself as a victim, or she could direct her energy and thoughts toward letting go of her past and trying to reinvent herself. She signed up for a 12-week professional skill-building program that taught her how to make a better life by believing in herself, putting her best face forward, and not letting her homelessness define her. She learned to craft a résumé, dress respectfully, communicate professionally, and ace an interview.

Although their shelter usually only allowed people to stay for six months, the administrators were so impressed with how hard Helen and her husband were working that they allowed them to stay for a year. During this time both Helen and her husband secured full-time jobs and were eventually able to find a two-bedroom apartment that they could afford on their own.

Helen recently had the opportunity to share her inspirational story at a fund-raising gala for Wardrobe for Opportunity, a charity that provides suitable clothing to people who need it to secure a job. A guest at the gala was so inspired by Helen's presence and fortitude that he recruited her to manage his spa. Helen is now earning $40,000 a year with benefits and paid vacation.

Since then, several other nonprofits have asked Helen to speak at their fund-raising events because her story is so uplifting. Helen has ambitions to write a book to inspire others who feel that their lives are hopeless. She feels incredibly abundant knowing that she has a powerful mind-set and the ability to overcome challenges that could seem insurmountable.

Despite the horrific experience of being homeless, Helen feels deep gratitude for all that she received: the therapy, the career training, and the insight that she didn't want to end up feeling victimized the rest of her life. She was forced to look within. There, she found the source of her true wealth—the conviction that she *had* enough and that she *was* enough.

Helen saw very clearly that she didn't want to accept a life of poverty and instability. She chose to focus on her future instead of her past, finding the support she needed to reframe her beliefs until she finally felt *worthy*. She believed she could create a better life for herself and her family. And she did it.

I asked Helen, "If I told you one year ago that your family would be living in your own apartment, and that you'd have a household income of $75,000 a year, would you have believed it?"

She was thoughtful and replied, "No way. I never dreamed my life would turn out this way. I didn't believe my life could change this much so quickly—but my beliefs changed."

I asked her how satisfied she is with her life today. She yelled out a resounding "10" as we hooted and hollered, joyfully celebrating her journey from scarcity into abundance.

You Have to Apply Yourself

Helen's story has many lessons in it, and one is that the path to abundance isn't always smooth. It's not like you will suddenly leap into the Abundance Loop in the blink of an eye and stay there happily and joyfully for the rest of your days. No, like Helen, it might take months or years of incremental gains before you can plan a party and truthfully say, "I made it out. I broke free."

What really happens is that as you try to get a handle on your insecurities, you will naturally waffle back and forth quite a bit at the beginning. Fears and ego are always there, harassing you for trying something new, intent on convincing you that nothing will ever change. But eventually if you apply yourself, your self-confidence will increase; the system will click in; and before long, you'll see something minor happen, something positive you didn't expect, and it will give you the confidence to persevere. Eventually it gets easier, and abundance gradually becomes more evident in all aspects of your life. How great is that? It works.

But then what? Just when you least expect it, a crushing loss, grief situation, or illness could hit you like a ton of bricks—that's just part of life. What will save you the second time around, or the third or fourth times? *The resiliency that you developed the first time you struggled through the process.* The difference now is that you won't give up in the face of sudden adversity because in your heart, you know you are worthy of your life. This time if you get struck down, you have steps you can follow, concrete techniques, and an A-Team to help you get yourself back in tune with your own divine abundance.

Another scenario is also possible. What if you just pay lip service to this theory and don't really apply yourself? You rush through the book, halfheartedly trying only a few of the exercises. You read the last chapter and wonder why you lack conscious wealth. Fear seeps in, and it makes you think: *This will never work for me. This stuff never works.* Your frustration then leads you to complain, and in your anger and impatience, you end up feeling unhappy about the whole thing.

But truly, why did this process not work for you? Did you make an honest attempt to cultivate awareness and adjust your beliefs? Did you practice expressing gratitude for what you already have? Did you take time to add up your resources and your expenses and take conscious action based on that analysis? No? Well, guess what? You're still stuck in a Scarcity Loop, only it looks something like this:

It's not the end of the world, just another lesson. What if you maybe read through the steps again, but this time, make a genuine effort to do the exercises and understand the content. What do you have to lose? Shoot to live in the Abundance Loop and, with some time and effort, the following experience can be yours. *Why wait any longer?*

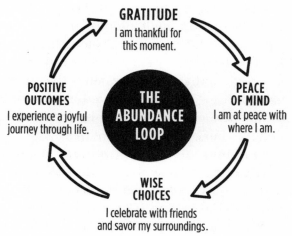

Appreciate Your True Abundance

Fifty-year-old Ron would be the first one to caution you not to wait too long to make a change in your life. His story is about how his drive to be CFO (chief financial officer) was almost his downfall. Ron was a high achiever beginning in grade school. He graduated from an Ivy League college, finishing at the top of his class at one of the best business schools in the country. He landed a great job and was in a race to the top.

But Ron refused to relax until he hit senior management and his total compensation surpassed a million a year. He complained openly and often about others who he thought weren't nearly as smart as he was yet who networked their way into better jobs. His jealousy and resentment blocked him from celebrating other people's achievements and fueled him to work even harder, with longer hours and more travel. His incessant quest for more and more hampered his personal life; sometimes he felt like a stranger in his own home because he was there so infrequently. Plus his frustration about not rising quickly enough at work cast a cloud on his enjoyment of other aspects of his life.

Today, Ron looks back and deeply regrets missing out on time with his children when they were younger, not being there more for his wife, and letting his friendships slide. He finally hit his target of being CFO with a million-dollar package, but now he can see that he was actually wealthy all along because his family stood by him. Had he done a values exercise earlier in his career, he would have realized that his family tied at the top of his list of values, along with his work, and he would have shifted the allocation of his time and energy. He could have celebrated his true wealth all along . . . but better late than never.

He has since adjusted his priorities, devoting more quality time to his two sons, getting to know them better before they head off to college. Ron and his wife even signed up for swing-dancing lessons twice a week and are getting to know each other all over again. Each date together is like a celebration of their lives, and they are grateful that their marriage made it through the last 20 years.

EXERCISE:
Celebrate Your Abundance

Abundance is within you and around you 24/7, so you can celebrate this fact any day and every day, morning, noon, or night. There is so much to celebrate in life and so many easy and fun ways to do it. Celebrate each step along your abundance journey. This exercise gives you some ideas to get you started. I invite you to add more of your own. Be as creative as you want—really open up your mind to possibility. Then read back over the full list and make a commitment to do at least one or more of these activities every day, to consciously celebrate your abundant life.

How Can You Celebrate Your Health Today?

- Can you go for a walk or run?

- Do some light yoga?

- Dance after dinner for 20 minutes?

- Hit the gym?

How Can You Celebrate Your Finances?

- Can you plant a real tree in celebration of your beginning your own Money Tree?

- Increase your monthly contributions?

- Share the news when you've paid down your debt?

- Make cookies for your financial advisor? (I like this idea!)

How Can You Celebrate Your Family?

- Can you take the time to read a story with your children?

- Go for a walk with them?

- Cook a nice, healthy dinner? Maybe add a candle on the table?

- Start a new family tradition that happens on the first of every month?

How Can You Celebrate the Positive Progress in Your Life?

- Can you treat yourself to dessert and coffee at your favorite café?

- Do some daydreaming about your next big personal project?

- Design a vision board with images and phrases that you draw or cut out from magazines?

- Share your story as an example to friends and then offer to support them in finding their way out of scarcity?

Coming Out and Into Your Divine Self

Divine abundance is not just about money—as you know, it's about abundance in all aspects of our human existence. Living the truth of who you are is critical if you wish to reach your full potential and manifest conscious wealth.

I interviewed my friend Peter, whose story illustrates this principle in a very poignant way. Peter knew since he was a teenager that he was attracted to men. But being gay was at odds with his Christian faith. He repressed his sexual instincts, took on a leadership role in his church, built a successful business, got married, and had two wonderful children.

At 52, Peter had achieved all the markers of success financially and socially, but he was far from content. He suffered serious depression and considered taking his life. More money, success, or recognition could not fulfill his deepest desire. He desperately wanted to express who he truly was on the inside.

With the support of close friends, counselors, and his pastor, he decided to come out as a gay man. He was humbled to discover that not only did other people accept his sexual orientation, but he had also learned to accept himself. With immense gratitude, he started a foundation to support others who want to come out and celebrate their true selves. Peter is now committed to ending prejudice and offering resources to those who are still living in fear and darkness about their sexual orientation.

Today, as a high-functioning executive, Peter has found balance between his inner self and his outer world. By believing that he is enough just as he is, he is able to manifest his Divine Self in this world. He lives a life that reflects his true identity, and he uses the financial wealth that he accumulated to serve a purpose that is dear to his heart . . . helping others come out into the light.

Achieving a Healthy Balance

We can see from Peter's story the importance of aligning all aspects of our lives with our deepest personal values. You will find that reaching a true point of balance between your inner self and who you show to the world will bring you more abundance in all other aspects of life, including financially, physically, and spiritually. Satisfied with what you have and who you are, you develop the confidence to go for what your heart desires. Once you start to experience abundance, more abundance naturally follows.

A balanced financial life requires that you plan ahead and take consistent action to manifest your goals. A balanced spiritual life requires you to watch for times when your scarcity mind-set may try to kick in. When it does, notice it. By simply witnessing your emotional state, you harness your power to be the agent of control and effect change. It's not about staying in the Abundance Loop, but knowing that you are divine and can easily navigate between the loops.

One main benefit of this approach is that when you find balance, your life moves forward with less of the struggle of push and pull, because you have broken free from the grip of your ego. You no longer repress your fears, nor do you obsess about your wants and needs. Your consciousness liberates you from your fears and desires. You have achieved the freedom to live an authentic life. Finally, you are free to be you. And that is what you can now celebrate: *the freedom to be you.*

EXERCISE:
Affirmations for Conscious Wealth

Affirmation statements are a popular way to remind yourself of the new, positive thoughts and beliefs that you're adopting as you move forward into your conscious wealth. Affirmations should always be stated in present tense. Even if you don't yet feel these things are true in your life at this time, say them as if they are already a fact. Your inner self hears them and feels them, and then those new patterns of behavior and abundance manifest in your world.

Repetition is especially important if you want to replace negative thought patterns from your past. You can say affirmations out loud in front of a mirror, and that is very effective, if you have time to do it two or three times a day or more. It is also powerful to make a recording of yourself reading the statements in your own voice. Record yourself repeating them

10 or 20 times each through your iPhone or computer. Listen to these affirmations as frequently as you can. The messages are personal to you, so play them through headphones if you don't want others around you to undermine your efforts.

The suggested affirmations below are to get you started and specifically reinforce the messages from *The Abundance Loop*. Feel free to add additional statements that are meaningful to you, but make sure to state them as personal, positive, and in the present tense. Record your personal affirmations that will manifest whatever abundance means to you in all areas of your life.

I Affirm Eight Promises to Myself to Celebrate My Abundant Life

I am abundant right now, and more continues to flow. Every time I put my ego aside and align with my Divine Self, following the Abundance Loop steps, I manifest financial security and spiritual serenity. I manifest conscious wealth.

1. *I choose to let go of fear. I am free.*

2. *I believe that I have enough and that I am enough. I am divine.*

3. *I give thanks for all that I have and for all that I experience. I am grateful.*

4. *I spend my time and money in alignment with my core values. I am living with purpose.*

5. *I track my cash flow and energy flow. I am aware of my financial and spiritual resources.*

6. *I commit to increasing my net worth and my self-worth. I am worthy.*

7. *I connect and collaborate with others to co-create an abundant world. I am connected.*

8. *I celebrate each step of my journey and the abundance of now. I am present.*

Take time out to celebrate. It's important. Celebrate each step you've taken to manifest conscious wealth. Celebrate that you are enough. In fact, you are more than enough—you are divine. The final equation I leave you with is this:

Your Divine Self = Abundance

Remember, your Divine Self is the inner you, your wise soul, the one that never lets you down.

Celebrate all that you have and all that you are. Celebrate all that you have to share with this world. Celebrate your Abundance Loop!

AFTERWORD

In the process of writing this book, I had to live through and practice the eight steps to manifest my own divine wealth. As afraid as I was to look within and resurrect old wounds, I could no longer withstand the torture of not being free to be me. I discovered my self-limiting belief that I was not enough. I see now that was just a clever way for my ego to keep me in its clutches and trap me in the Scarcity Loop. By meditating and repeating affirmations on a regular basis, I could quiet my mind and simply observe what was going on around me as well as within me. I felt overwhelming gratitude for everything from running water and food on the table to a loving family and so much more.

With the power of awareness, I was able to shift from fear to gratitude, from scarcity to abundance. I saw how truly blessed I was, but more important, I saw how truly blessed everyone else is as well. But when we're stuck in scarcity, we can't see the divine abundance that is rightfully ours.

As I took stock of my financial and spiritual wealth, including all the knowledge and experience I've gathered, how could I not align with my Divine Self? When it worked, how could I not share these insights? I made the choice to align with two of my core values, balance and communication, and created a series of seminars and workshops.

I am keenly interested in teaching both spiritual development concepts and financial wealth strategies, hence the name I gave my workshops is Conscious Wealth. By "conscious," I mean awareness: awareness of your thoughts, feelings, actions, reactions, and interactions. This also covers awareness of your physical behaviors, bodily sensations, emotional states, and mental habits. It's the awareness of what you are doing, thinking, and feeling, as well as the awareness of your relationship to yourself, to others, and to the world.

By now, you know that when I use the word *wealth,* I mean it as something that transcends money and encompasses all the blessings you have available to you that enrich your life, such as your health, family, friends, talents, and energy. Conscious wealth, then, is the awareness of the way you think, feel, and act with regard to your money, time, and inner and outer resources.

You can be conscious of the abundance that surrounds you and partake in the opportunities before you or remain in scarcity. It's your choice.

I hope you choose abundance. I hope you choose to manifest your divine wealth. That was my choice, and I look forward to spreading the word about how the Abundance Loop process and conscious wealth solutions can truly transform anyone's life.

With deepest gratitude,
Juliana

ENDNOTES

Step 3: Cultivate Gratitude

1. Emmons, R. A., and M. E. McCullough. "Counting blessings versus burdens: An experimental investigation of gratitude and subjective well-being in daily life." *Journal of Personality and Social Psychology*, 84(2), (2003): 377–389.

2. Lyubomirsky, Sonja, and Kennon Sheldon and David Schkade. Pursuing happiness: the architecture of sustainable change. *Review of General Psychology*, 9(2), (2005): 111–131.

3. Seligman, Martin. *Authentic Happiness: Using the New Positive Psychology to Realize Your Potential for Lasting Fulfillment.* New York. Simon & Schuster, 2002: 45.

Step 4: Clarify Your Values and Intentions

1. "The Transfer of Trust: Wealth and Succession in a Changing World." *Barclays Wealth Insights,* vol. 14, 2011.

2. Doran, George T. "There's a S.M.A.R.T. Way to Write Management's Goals and Objectives." *Management Review,* Nov. 1981.

RESOURCES

Conscious Wealth Resources: Access additional resources and practical tips, sign up for an upcoming workshop, or engage Juliana Park to speak at your organization's next event.

www.julianapark.com

Recommended Associations

Hay House I Can Do It!® Conference: www.hayhouse.com
Financial Peace University: www.daveramsey.com/fpu
Debtors Anonymous: www.debtorsanonymous.org
Underearners Anonymous: www.underearnersanonymous.org
Greater Good Science Center: http://greatergood.berkeley.edu

Highly Recommended Books

You Can Heal Your Life, by Louise Hay
Wishes Fulfilled, by Dr. Wayne W. Dyer
Nothing Changes Until You Do, by Mike Robbins
Money: Master the Game, by Tony Robbins
Think and Grow Rich, by Napoleon Hill
Affluence Intelligence, by Stephen Goldbart, Ph.D., and Joan Indursky DiFuria, MFT
A New Earth, by Eckhart Tolle
The Money Class, by Suze Orman
Smart Women Finish Rich, by David Bach

The Soul of Money, by Lynne Twist
The Energy of Money, by Maria Nemeth, Ph.D.
The Untethered Soul, by Michael A. Singer
The Law of Divine Compensation, by Marianne Williamson

APPENDIX

Adding a Financial Advisor
to Your A-Team

I highly recommend that you consider working with a financial advisor from your area and adding them to your A-Team (Abundance Team) as an ongoing resource. A good financial advisor can help you set your financial and personal goals, assess your current financial health, develop an action plan, and track your progress. There are thousands of advisors with different areas of expertise, and your job is to find one whom you trust and who suits your particular needs. Start by asking family and friends— people you respect and trust—and maybe your CPA or banker for referrals. Here are some questions to help you determine if a particular financial planner is a good fit for you:

- Do you trust this person to take care of you, your family, and your family's wealth?

- Does this person understand your fears, values, and personal and financial goals?

- How much experience does he or she have?

- Who else is on your advisor's team? (Different advisors have different areas of expertise, and many offer robust and efficient service models. Find out what each person does.)

- What is the planner's investment philosophy? What is his or her strategy, and how does he or she implement it? What financial instruments (such as funds, stocks, bonds, options, annuities, and so forth) does he or she use?

- What type of clients does he or she work with? What is the average or median size of clients' portfolios? Does he or she require a minimum amount to get started?

- What are the total fees, including underlying expenses?

- How does he or she get paid? On a commission basis, where he or she gets paid to sell you a product, or on a fee basis, where he or she gets paid a percentage of your assets to advise you?

- What credentials does he or she have?

Advisors who hold the Certified Financial Planner (CFP®) designation are dedicated to the financial-planning process and have met the education, experience, examination, and ethics requirements to help you achieve your financial goals. To find a CFP® professional in your area, you can use the planner search on the Financial Planning Association website: www.onefpa.org.

INDEX OF 30 EXERCISES

ACKNOWLEDGMENTS

It took a divine village to birth this book, and I could not have written it without the love, support, and guidance of many who have shared their wisdom, stories, and talent.

Reid Tracy and the Hay House staff, thank you for believing in my message and publishing my first book! When I went to your I Can Do It!® Conference in 2012, I knew I had finally come home. Louise Hay, Wayne Dyer, and your amazing cadre of authors always inspire me to look within and trust that a higher power is weaving through as I share my divine gift with others.

To my amazing editorial team: Thank you for being my writing angels! Christian de Quincey, for laying the groundwork. Ann Moller, for your loving guidance. Sari Friedman, for rescuing my manuscript. Simone Graham, thank you for jumping into the trenches, integrating all the pieces with your deep wisdom, and finally helping me deliver this bundle of joy and abundance!

Hay House Senior Editor Alex Freemon, thank you for your divine insights and your incredible patience!

I want to send a huge shout-out to the professors, staff, and classmates at John F. Kennedy University School of Holistic Studies who taught me to lean into my shadow and discover real wealth. Thank you for teaching me how to integrate all the facets of my identity and grounding me with confidence and skills so that I may be of the utmost service to this world.

Bob Lew, Joan DiFuria, and Dr. Stephen Goldbart, thank you for sharing your message: Values before money. Riley E. and Renee A., thank you for the training and opportunities. Clients, thank you for showing me the Abundance Loop in action.

Megan McNealy, thank you for being my spiritual sister as we both juggle family, career, health, and our passion to heal the world. Huge hugs to my greatest cheerleaders, Jared Anderson, Loyd Auerbach, Erina Buckley, Terry Chi, Ann Kennedy Coiteaux, DeAngela Cooks, Joe Diliberto, Peter Drake, Maggie Franco, Marilyn Fowler, Christopher Grady, Francinelee Hand, Deborah Jackson, Karen Jaenke, Mary Lee, Lindsay Meyer, Michelle Moquin, Tracy Murphy, Cheryl Pitts, Kerry Resch, Mike Robbins, Nancy Rothstein, Matt Schmitz, John Souza, Vernice Solimar, Sally Srok, Ingrid Stabb, Asha Stokes, Peter Vongphakdy, Ravneet Vohra, Claire Weber, Deborah Wood, and the Visionaries.

Thank you to my healers, Maya Bose, Juliana Damon, Vicki Dello Joio, Phyllis Klaus, Christine Lee, Abigail Surasky, and Roslyn Whitney, for aligning my body, mind, and soul.

My A-Team: Peter Ashbaugh, Jacky Carleton, Debra Amador DeLaRosa, Sarah Christensen Fu, Kate Montgomery, Lisa Wood, and Wendy Zito, thank you for manifesting Conscious Wealth with me!

My Conscious Wealth community: Thank you for showing up in my life and fueling my commitment to be of service!

Susan, David, and Eui-Ran, thank you for stepping up whenever I needed you. I am truly blessed for all our experiences together and your unconditional love. Mom and Dad, thank you for always loving me and teaching me to be grateful for all that I have. Halmuni, thank you for modeling that there's always enough to share.

Sasha, Aaron, Sterling, my divine children, I love you. Thank you for serving as living reminders that love and abundance surrounds me every moment! Elizabeth Hale, nanny from heaven, thank you for being our Mary Poppins.

My dearest husband and soul mate, Christopher, thank you for loving me patiently and supporting me to align with my divine. I love you and being by your side on this abundant journey.

Readers, I am bursting with love and gratitude for all of you. Thank you for co-creating an abundant world together with me. Thank you for being you.

ABOUT THE AUTHOR

Juliana Park, CFP®, is passionate about helping people break free from the Scarcity Loop and live in the Abundance Loop. She developed a series of Conscious Wealth seminars and courses to transform people's relationships with money, with others, and with themselves.

Juliana has been advising wealthy families for more than 13 years. She is currently a vice president at a global financial institution. A Certified Financial Planner, Juliana holds an MBA from the Yale School of Management, and she went on to earn her MA in Integral Psychology at John F. Kennedy University. She also has a Bachelor of Fine Arts degree from the Cooper Union School of Art. Juliana won the Hay House Writer's Workshop nonfiction contest in 2012.

Juliana lives an abundant life in Northern California with her husband and three children. She is committed to co-creating an abundant world with you.

For more information, please visit www.julianapark.com.

We hope you enjoyed this Hay House book.
If you'd like to receive our online catalog featuring
additional information on Hay House books and products,
or if you'd like to find out more about the
Hay Foundation, please contact:

Hay House, Inc., P.O. Box 5100, Carlsbad, CA 92018-5100
(760) 431-7695 or (800) 654-5126
(760) 431-6948 (fax) or (800) 650-5115 (fax)
www.hayhouse.com® • www.hayfoundation.org

Published and distributed in Australia by: Hay House Australia Pty. Ltd.,
18/36 Ralph St., Alexandria NSW 2015
Phone: 612-9669-4299 • *Fax:* 612-9669-4144 • www.hayhouse.com.au

Published and distributed in the United Kingdom by: Hay House UK, Ltd.,
Astley House, 33 Notting Hill Gate, London W11 3JQ
Phone: 44-20-3675-2450 • *Fax:* 44-20-3675-2451 • www.hayhouse.co.uk

Published and distributed in the Republic of South Africa by:
Hay House SA (Pty), Ltd., P.O. Box 990, Witkoppen 2068 • info@hayhouse.co.za

Published in India by: Hay House Publishers India,
Muskaan Complex, Plot No. 3, B-2, Vasant Kunj, New Delhi 110 070
Phone: 91-11-4176-1620 • *Fax:* 91-11-4176-1630 • www.hayhouse.co.in

Distributed in Canada by: Raincoast Books,
2440 Viking Way, Richmond, B.C. V6V 1N2
Phone: 1-800-663-5714 • *Fax:* 1-800-565-3770 • www.raincoast.com

Take Your Soul on a Vacation

Visit www.HealYourLife.com® to regroup,
recharge, and reconnect with your own magnificence.
Featuring blogs, mind-body-spirit news, and
life-changing wisdom from Louise Hay and friends.

Visit www.HealYourLife.com today.